PRIMER contents

growing
gospel-driven
churches

fiec the **FELLOWSHIP** *of* **INDEPENDENT EVANGELICAL CHURCHES**

Primer is produced by the Fellowship of Independent Evangelical Churches (FIEC); a family of churches in Britain, working together to go and make disciples of Jesus Christ in every community. Find out more at *fiec.org.uk*

> *"The righteousness of God is our standing-place in the air – that is to say, where there is no human possibility of standing – whose foundations are laid by God Himself and supported always by Him only."*

Karl Barth, *The Epistle to the Romans*, trans. Edwyn C. Hoskyns (Oxford: Oxford University Press, 1933), 93.

I love that image of justification. On the one hand it captures the way that we have no leg to stand on; no ground to stand on, even, before God. As Barth says, human unrighteousness and ungodliness mean that there is no human possibility of standing.

On the other hand, it captures the security of our position. We have a standing place in the air, and it has foundations. It's a striking and impossible image but it's wonderful: against all odds God has recreated the human situation. He has done the impossible. He has given sinful people a secure place to stand before him.

This issue of *Primer* will take plenty of time to spell that out and work through its implications. For now though, I want to set a tone and explain the contents.

First, the tone. One of the reasons for taking justification as a theme is that it is simply so good. As Steve Timmis puts it later in *Primer*, it is "cosmically joyful." You can hear the wonder in that Barth quote. Straight after it, Barth quotes Luther who describes the announcement of God's righteousness as "the sermon of sermons and the wisdom of heaven." In Luther's own account of his conversion, it was after grasping the offer of the gift of God's righteousness that "I felt that I had been born anew and that the gates of heaven had been opened."

Wherever the doctrine of justification has been grasped, joy has overflowed. An unknown author from the second century A.D. gushes in praise at the thought of it:

From *Epistle to Diognetus*.

> *O, the surpassing kindness and love of God! He did not hate us, or reject us, or bear a grudge against us; instead He was patient and forbearing. In His mercy He took upon Himself our sins. He Himself gave up His own Son as a ransom for us, the holy one for the lawless, the guiltless for the guilty, the just for the unjust, the incorruptible for the corruptible, the immortal for the mortal.*
>
> *For what else but His righteousness could have covered our sins? In whom was it possible for us, the lawless and ungodly, to be justified, except in the Son of God alone?*
>
> *O the sweet exchange, O the incomprehensible work of God, O the unexpected blessings, that the sinfulness of many should be hidden in one righteous person, while the righteousness of One should justify many sinners!*

Or picture the poet and hymn-writer William Cowper, who was committed to the St. Albans Insane Asylum but in December 1763 found a Bible on a bench. He took it up and read Romans 3:25, and later records this in his memoir:

Apparently, the doctor in charge used to leave them lying around for people to find.

> *Immediately I received the strength to believe it, and the full beams of the Sun of Righteousness shone upon me. I saw the sufficiency of the atonement He had made, my pardon sealed in His blood, and all the fullness and completeness of His justification. In a moment I believed, and received the gospel... Unless the Almighty arm had been under me, I think I should have died with gratitude and joy. My eyes filled with tears, and my voice choked with transport; I could only look up to heaven in silent fear, overwhelmed with love and wonder.*

So, the aim of this issue of *Primer* is to help us to feel something of that, to *enjoy* this doctrine. For that reason we will keep circling around the questions of what it means and what difference it makes in the Christian life.

Second, the contents. We have crafted this issue to help us enjoy the doctrine, but also in the recognition that when people hear the word *justification* they don't always think of a joyful standing place. Throughout church history justification has been disputed and it can seem that the doctrine is now clouded by theological debate and tarnished by historical divisions. So we want to address that head on. We have asked the church historian and theologian Matthew Barrett to give us an overview of justification debates from the early church to the Reformation to help us understand why Luther thought the doctrine was worth taking a stand for. Matthew gives us something that's very hard to find: an 800 year survey that helps us put some big concepts in place and introduces us to some major figures in the history of the doctrine.

According to legend, when Luther was called to appear before the Holy Roman Emperor to defend his views on justification he boldly proclaimed, *"Here I stand; I can do no other. God help me."*

It's doubtful he ever said those words, but he is recorded as saying something similar:

"I consider myself convicted by the testimony of Holy Scripture, which is my basis; my conscience is captive to the Word of God. Thus I cannot and will not recant, because acting against one's conscience is neither safe nor sound. God help me. Amen."

Then, we'll jump ahead 200 years or so and meet John Owen, who saw that justification by faith was a precious source of comfort and so took up the fight in his day. Owen is known as the "Prince of the Puritans." He is certainly one of the greatest theologians of that age, but he can be intimidating to read, so we have asked Paul Gibson to annotate, explain and apply John Owen for today. With Paul's notes to ease you in, it may just be the start of a beautiful friendship.

Of course the most famous division about justification happened at the Reformation, where the Protestants split from the Roman Catholic church. In 2017 we reach a significant anniversary in Luther's life (it is 500 years since he first launched his protest by nailing his 95 theses to a church door), but you can be sure that many will find no cause for celebration. Increasingly, the Reformation is seen as a tragic rift in the church caused by debates which were never or are no longer necessary. Gregg Allison's article, however, spells out the ongoing differences between a Protestant and Catholic understanding of salvation. In a conversation that so often falls into caricatures or papers over significant differences, Gregg gives a clear summary of both the Catholic and the Protestant positions.

More recently, the traditional Reformed reading of justification has been challenged by several movements in New Testament studies, such as the 'New Perspective.' Many of us might know there's a debate but not have had the time to work out what it all means and what difference it makes. You might have even tried to wrap your head around that complicated debate and come away more confused still. Well, help is at hand! David Starling summarises and reflects on the debates of the last 50 years, distilling the implications for pastors and teachers. He is a sure guide through some rocky terrain and worth following carefully if you want to get a handle on why those debates matter.

The last two articles also have pastors and teachers firmly in view. One of the perennial accusations against justification by faith is that it is an individualistic doctrine, teaching us only to care about 'me and my standing before God.' And yet, as my article explores, justification is closely related to mission, church unity, suffering and a host of other themes in Scripture. So we will have a chance to trace the many ways in which Jesus and Paul develop the applications of justification by faith. And then finally, Steve Timmis helps us think about how to teach justification. He identifies some of the reasons people find it hard to believe and shares some ideas and resources to help us all treasure and teach the doctrine of justification by faith.

DAVID SHAW is the Editor of *Primer*. He is part-time Theological Adviser for FIEC and part-time lecturer in New Testament and Greek at Oak Hill Theological College, London. He's married to Jo and they have four children.

 @_david_shaw

GREGG R. ALLISON is professor of Christian theology at The Southern Baptist Theological Seminary. He is the author of *Historical Theology: An Introduction to Christian Doctrine*, *Sojourners and Strangers: The Doctrine of the Church*, and *Roman Catholic Theology and Practice: An Evangelical Assessment*.

MATTHEW BARRETT is Tutor of Systematic Theology and Church History at Oak Hill College in London, as well as the founder and executive editor of Credo Magazine. He is the author of several books, including *Salvation by Grace*, *Owen on the Christian Life*, *God's Word Alone: The Authority of Scripture*, and *Reformation Theology*.

PAUL GIBSON serves as a pastor at Wheelock Heath Baptist Church in south Cheshire. He studied History at Oxford University and Theological and Pastoral Studies at Oak Hill College, including a Masters Dissertation looking at the doctrine of justification in John Owen and Richard Baxter.

JOHN OWEN was married to Mary and they had 11 children, 10 of whom tragically died in infancy. He was an English Nonconformist church leader, theologian, and the author of many works, including *Communion with God*, *The Mortification of Sin*, *The Glory of Christ: His Office and his Grace*, and *The Death of Death in the Death of Christ*.

DAVID STARLING lives in Sydney, Australia, with his wife Nicole and their four children, and teaches New Testament at Morling College. He worked as a high school English teacher before completing theological studies and serving as a pastor in Sydney's inner-western suburbs. He is currently writing commentaries on Colossians, Ephesians and 1 Corinthians.

STEVE TIMMIS is CEO of Acts 29 and lives in Sheffield where he is the Senior Elder in The Crowded House. He is married to Janet and they have four children and 10 grandchildren. He lives in a house with four generations and a dog! He has co-authored a number of books as well as managing to write a couple all on his own.

back to the truth

a history
of grace and
justification
from Augustine
to Luther

by Matthew
Barrett

The Protestant Reformers of the sixteenth century believed that the doctrine of justification by grace alone through faith alone was absolutely central to the Christian faith. They were convinced, however, that it was in desperate need of recovery.

But why?

What had been taught in the centuries that preceded the Reformation to persuade reformers like Martin Luther that the church of his day had largely misunderstood how a sinner is made right with God?

To answer that question, we will need to travel back in time and explore the contours of grace and justification as understood by individuals like Augustine, Thomas Aquinas, and Gabriel Biel. In doing so, we will begin to appreciate why Luther believed the church needed not merely a reformation in morality but most importantly a reformation in doctrine. As we'll see, that insight still has ongoing implications for Protestant Christians today.

When grace becomes law:
The Legacy of Pelagius

If anyone was well known for his religious zeal it was Pelagius. Living in Rome in the late fourth century, Pelagius became a student of the church fathers, which fuelled within him an incomparable passion for godliness. Yet passion for godliness can be a dangerous thing if it does not operate within a biblical understanding of salvation. The type of passion that characterised Pelagius led to a strict monastery life. Perfection was the goal. In part, Pelagius was motivated by a desire to reform the church. However, unlike the sixteenth century Protestant Reformers, the reform Pelagius heralded was a reform in morals, not primarily a reform in doctrine.

A reform in morality is commendable, but for Pelagius this reform assumed man had the inherent ability to reform himself before and, in some cases, even apart from supernatural grace. For example, in a letter Pelagius wrote to Demetrias one can sense that the stress of this moral reform falls upon man's natural power: "As often as I have to speak concerning moral improvement and the leading of a holy life, I am accustomed first to set forth the power and quality of human nature, and to show what it can accomplish." For Pelagius, the power of human nature can accomplish much. So much, in fact, that even after the Fall of Adam into sin mankind is able to follow God's commandments by means of his own power and ability. This explains why Pelagius dissented so viciously from Augustine's famous prayer in his *Confessions*: "Give what you command, and command what you will." What a contradiction, Pelagius protested. The will is not free if it needs God's help. Furthermore, God would not give us commands if we were unable to fulfil them. While grace may be helpful, it certainly is not absolutely necessary.

B. R. Rees, *The Letters of Pelagius and His Followers* (Rochester, NY: Boydell, 1991), 1:xiv.

Augustine, *Confessions*, trans. Maria Boulding, ed. John E. Rotelle, I/1 of The Works of Augustine (New York: New City, 1997), 10.40.

pelagius
c. 360-418

john cassian

augustine

Quoted by Augustine, *Nature and Grace*, in *Answer to the Pelagians I*, trans. Roland J. Teske, ed. John E. Rotelle, I/23 of *The Works of Augustine* (New York: New City, 1997), 10.

Underneath Pelagius' negative reaction to Augustine's prayer was his rejection of original sin. Pelagius believed mankind does not inherit from Adam either the guilt for his sin or his corrupt nature. What, we might ask, explains why the world is so evil? Pelagius' answer: man does not inherit Adam's corruption but merely mimics the bad examples he witnesses. The tragedy of Adam in Genesis 3, therefore, is not that all mankind is condemned as a result of Adam's representation, but rather that Adam was a terrible role model. This imitation view, as we might label it, is especially apparent in how Pelagius interprets Romans 5:12: "The statement that all have sinned in Adam was not uttered on account of a sin contracted by reason of their origin through being born, but on account of the imitation of Adam's sin." Nevertheless, humans are capable of resisting this habit to sin. Indeed, we are capable of not sinning at all, since we have not inherited Adam's sinful disposition nor are we necessarily inclined to sin.

Pelagius was convinced that his view could be supported by the entire storyline of the Bible. He divided the biblical story into three epochs:

> 1) **The epoch of nature:** From Adam to Moses many biblical characters (e.g. Abel, Noah, Melchizedek, Abraham, and Job) reached a state of perfection. This impressive accomplishment was due, Pelagius believed, to their adherence to the law of nature within them. Sadly, however, many others were unaware that this law of nature existed within, or they were aware but chose instead to follow the evil example of those around them.

> 2) **The epoch of the written law:** From Moses to Christ, God put his law into writing. Now the ignorant really had no excuse. The point of this written law, said Pelagius, was to bring enlightenment. In other words, the way to achieve eternal life was through the law, specifically the law's ability to enlighten one's mind concerning God's rules for holy living. In short, we can

be justified by obeying God's commands. If we are not justified it is not because we are spiritually incapable of obeying the law; instead, it is because we abandoned the law which was able to make us right with God. Grace, in this epoch at least, means God was kind enough to provide mankind with his law, the means to attaining a justified status.

3) **The epoch of the law of Christ:** In the days of Christ and the centuries that followed, mankind has repeatedly demonstrated that he enjoys sin. With God's written law being ignored, and therefore no longer sufficient for enlightenment, God deemed it necessary to send Christ so that this downward trajectory might be reversed. But Pelagius' interpretation of Christ's saving work is different than we might expect. Christ is Saviour in the sense that he brings a law that is greater than the law of Moses. Justification, we must notice, is still by means of God's law, but now one is justified by obeying Christ's commands, not those of Moses. Again, grace is law, but now it is found in a greater law. While mankind's plight took a wrong turn by following the example of Adam, now the plight can be reversed if only sinners follow the example of Christ.

On the surface, Pelagius sounds very biblical, perhaps even orthodox. He is no stranger to the word "grace," invoking its importance continually. Yet the discerning reader may have noticed that what Pelagius means by "grace" is not what one might assume. Pelagius has turned grace into law, and many in his day were quick to point this out. Although Pelagius attracted some followers, many of whom would be far more gifted at developing his theological views, Pelagius' theology would be condemned by the councils of Carthage (412), Constantinople (429), and Ephesus (431).

Somewhere in between:
Semi-Pelagianism

Theologians love to make distinctions. One distinction that has proved helpful in this discussion is the distinction between monergism and synergism. Monergism means there is but one actor, working alone, and working effectively. Synergism means there are two actors cooperating with one another, either successfully or unsuccessfully, depending upon whether one of the participants resists the other. Applied to our discussion, Augustine, as we will soon learn, is a monergist. Since mankind has inherited Adam's corrupt nature, he is spiritually dead and incapable of doing anything that might earn him right standing with God. God must do it all, causing him to be born again so that he will repent and believe. Though this may come as a surprise, Pelagius too can be labelled a monergist. Yet note the difference: while Augustine held to divine monergism, Pelagius' view could be labelled human monergism.

The situation became all the more complex when others, who have been labelled Semi-Pelagians, expressed their disagreement with both Pelagius and Augustine. John Cassian, Faustus of Riez, and Vincent of Lerins are just a few representatives. They were convinced that Pelagius had gone too far in his rejection of original sin. Humanity's sinfulness must be attributed to more than just a habit of imitation. Yet these Semi-Pelagians were not entirely sympathetic with Augustine either, for they did not believe mankind was so crippled by original sin that we are incapable of initiating salvation in the first place. For them, we do have a degree of spiritual ability prior to conversion and justification. Depravity is not so bad as to require an effectual, monergistic grace; we are able to start the salvation process. Nevertheless, original sin cannot be denied, so grace must be present, though this grace can be resisted in the synergistic event.

The Semi-Pelagian reaction is especially seen with the monks of Hadrumetum in Northern Africa. Like Pelagius, they too did not entirely

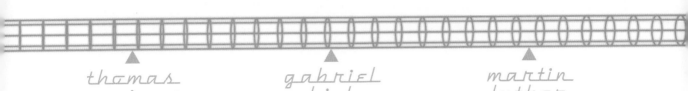

appreciate Augustine's writings, particularly his letter to Sixtus in 418. One monk by the name of Florus became irritated with Augustine's emphasis on sola gratia (grace alone), primarily because it seemed to undercut the monastic emphasis on self-discipline, which relied significantly upon the free will of mankind. Other monks reacted strongly as well, including Cresconius and Felix who met with Augustine but remained unpersuaded. Augustine responded with his famous work, *Grace and Free Will*, not only asserting the primacy of grace in conversion but also claiming that it was God's grace that sustained man entirely, enabling him to persevere in the Christian life. This teaching was not received well. One monk claimed that Augustine's logic would undermine man's culpability for sin. In his response, *Rebuke and Grace*, Augustine clarified that he was not denying human moral agency. Yet he was stressing the biblical theme of divine sovereignty: God must be the first to act upon the unconverted and he must do so effectually. If not, we will never turn away from sin and turn to Christ. We cannot act, in other words, unless we are first acted upon.

Monks in Southern France joined the Semi-Pelagian fold as well, claiming that apart from God's help human beings can take the first steps towards God, initiating salvation. These monks motivated Augustine to write two more books: *The Predestination of the Saints* and *The Gift of Perseverance*. Augustine's theological strength was met, however, by John Cassian, who knew Pelagius when he was in Rome and who took offence at Augustine's belief in effectual grace. According to Cassian, it is "when God sees us inclined to will what is good," that he then "meets, guides, and strengthens us."

John Cassian, *The Conferences*, trans. Boniface Ramsey, Ancient Christian Writers, 57 (New York: Newman, 1997), 13.9.

Despite its resolute advocates, the Synod of Orange (529) and the Synod of Valence (in the same year) would condemn Semi-Pelagianism. Yet it would be a mistake to think they fully embraced Augustine's position. Original sin, they concluded, has a very strong grip, so strong that we cannot initiate salvation or justification. God's grace must come first. However, God's grace is an *enabling* grace; it does not work monergistically but synergistically. Though it comes first, we must decide whether we will embrace it in the end.

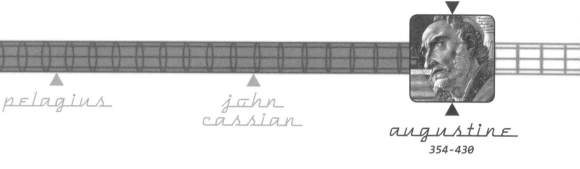

The graciousness of grace:
Augustine

Readers may be surprised to discover that at the start of Augustine's career he held a very different view of grace than he would in his debates with the Pelagians and Semi-Pelagians later on. In his books *On Free Will* and *The Happy Life*, Augustine attributes a spiritual ability to free will, though later in life, as seen in his *Retractions*, Augustine would regret his early elevation of free will over grace.

While the *Confessions* may have been one of the sparks that moved Pelagius to react so strongly to Augustine, the reverse cannot be said of Augustine. Long before the controversy, perhaps around 400 A.D., Augustine was already developing his mature understanding of grace in conversion. As he wrote his *Confessions*, Augustine reflected on passages like Romans 9 where the apostle firmly exalts unconditional grace in predestination, especially in contrast to the desperate depravity and inability of the sinner. The Pelagian controversy would then bring Augustine's conclusions into polemical focus like never before.

For Augustine, Adam was created sinless. His will, it follows, was not yet enslaved to sin but free to obey the Creator. Adam's fellowship with God in the garden involved his whole being, body and soul. The possibility of not sinning (the Latin phrase is *posse non peccare*) was very real, though we should not assume this entailed the impossibility of sinning (*non posse peccare*). Not so after Genesis 3 unfortunately. Giving way to pride for the first time, Adam was persuaded by the lying serpent, distrusting the promises of God. Due to the organic union between Adam and all the little Adams to follow, Adam's first sinful choice would result in his children receiving both his guilt and his corrupt nature. This infection was not limited to one part of human nature but its poison spread to every corner of our being, including the recesses of the will. The pollution of sin, in other words, lacked prejudice, enslaving each of our faculties. Whereas before the fall there was no necessity to sin, the same could not be said after being expelled from the garden. Now, unlike before, the will is not able not to sin (*non posse non peccare*).

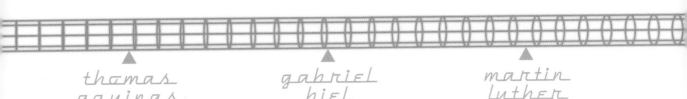

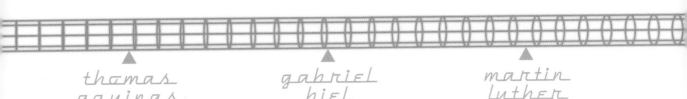thomas aquinas   gabriel biel   martin luther

This inability immediately eliminates both Pelagianism and Semi-Pelagianism and demands a different view of grace entirely. Grace cannot be optional or merely assisting; it is now necessary and must be the first thing to work omnipotently. Grace, Augustine asserts, "makes known to people what they ought to do, but also enables them to perform with love the duty that they know." In contrast to Pelagius, knowledge of one's duty is terribly insufficient; it assumes the unregenerate person is capable of something when he is actually capable of nothing, spiritually speaking. Augustine complained that the Pelagians "wish to say that the law is grace" when the "true meaning of grace is the love that God breathes into us, which enables us with a holy delight to carry out the duty that we know." Grace, Augustine concluded, is not "bestowed on man because he already believes, but that he may believe; not because he has deserved it by good works, but that he may deserve good works." This order between grace and good works means that justification must be *sola gratia*.

For Augustine, the gift of grace consists of an "effectual call," which is another way of saying he was a divine monergist. While the gospel may be preached to all, nevertheless, the Spirit works specifically within the hearts of those whom God has elected. His call is irresistibly sweet, causing new life to sprout within. Faith and repentance follow this effectual call and new birth (i.e. regeneration). Both are gifts from God: not gifts God offers in the hope we will accept, but gifts God actually works within us, ensuring that we will repent and believe. And all this is absolutely necessary in view of the unregenerate person's pervasive depravity and spiritual inability.

Augustine would qualify, however, that this irresistible grace is not coercive. Yes it works effectually upon our will but it does so not by violating it but by liberating it from its sinful bondage so that we willingly trust in the Saviour. Or to use more Augustinian vocabulary, God's grace is *prevenient* (arriving prior to conversion, preparing the sinner for future change) and *operative* (causing conversion; i.e. God operating upon the sinner); it's only after conversion that grace becomes *cooperative*, working with the renewed will to bring about a holy life.

Augustine, *A Treatise on Rebuke and Grace*, 3, in *Answer to the Pelagians, IV*, ed. John E. Rotelle, I/26 of *The Works of Saint Augustine*, ed. Roland J. Teske (New York: New City, 1997-1999), 110.

Augustine, *Answer to the Two Letters of the Pelagians*, 4, in *Answer to the Pelagians, II*, ed. John E. Rotelle, I/24 of *The Works of Saint Augustine*, ed. Roland J. Teske (New York: New City, 1997-1999), 11.

For a basic introduction to these three categories, see Alister E. McGrath, *Christian Theology: An Introduction*, Fifth ed. (Oxford: Wiley-Blackwell, 2011), 356.

pelagius

john
cassian

augustine

Augustine is praised by Protestants today for his tireless resistance against the very real threat of Pelagianism and Semi-Pelagianism in the church. Yet, despite Augustine's emphasis on *sola gratia*, it would be mistaken to label him a "Protestant" before there was Protestantism. The Reformers themselves readily acknowledge this point, praising Augustine's defence of *sola gratia* but expressing their disagreement with his formulation of justification itself. On the one hand, Augustine did teach that man is not justified by his good works but rather is given a righteousness from God. Nevertheless, a difference appears precisely at this point. While the Reformers would affirm an alien righteousness which is *imputed* to our account, Augustine taught that the righteousness God graciously gives is *imparted*, meaning that the sinner is not counted or declared forensically (legally) righteous, but actually *made* righteous.

This is to confuse aspects of "sanctification" (the Spirit's progressive inner renewal of the believer into the image of Christ by which he/she is made holy) with "justification" (i.e. on the basis of Christ's obedience being imputed to the believer's account, God makes a legal declaration that one is no longer guilty but righteous).

David F. Wright, "Justification in Augustine," in *Justification in Perspective: Historical Developments and Contemporary Challenges* (Grand Rapids: Baker Academic, 2006), 70. Or as Augustine himself said in one of his sermons, "We have been justified, but *justitia* [i.e. our righteousness/justified-ness] itself grows as we progress." *Sermon* 158.4-5 (*PL* 38:864-65). *PL = Patrologia Latina*, ed. J.P. Migne, 217 vols. (Paris, 1844-1864).

Sermon 159.1.1 (*PL* 38:367-68).

To be fair, Augustine was not ignorant that there was a legal dimension to justification. Historians and theologians now acknowledge that Augustine did at times incorporate a legal dimension to the justification event. Nevertheless, in the end justification is, as David Wright observes, both an "event and process, as both beginning and growth." While justification is something that has happened, it is also something that is unfinished, only partly complete. As long as the Christian sins he is only "partly justified." For this

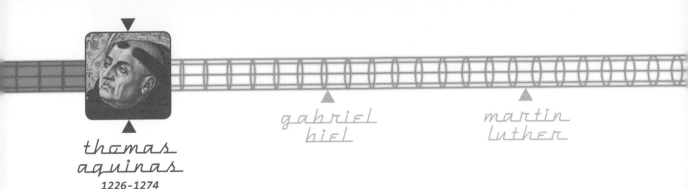

reason, David Wright warns us about getting ahead of ourselves. We must be careful that in our excitement over Augustine's affirmation of *sola gratia* we do not then assume the intricacies of his doctrine of justification are the same as later Reformers. Augustine and John Calvin, for example, did not mean the same thing when they referred to the word 'justification,' despite how much Calvin celebrated Augustine's belief in the graciousness of justification itself.

Wright, "Justification in Augustine," 71-72.

The medieval vortex:
From Thomas Aquinas to Gabriel Biel

In the medieval era discussions over grace and justification would come into sharper focus. While we cannot survey the vast canon of medieval thinkers here, we should pay attention to some key representatives and their distinctives. Arguably the most important medieval theologian is Thomas Aquinas (1226-1274) who wrote a colossal theology called the *Summa Theologiae*.

In his *Summa*, Aquinas is not shy to make fine distinctions concerning the nature of grace. To learn to appreciate them, we first must identify a philosophical commitment that sat quietly behind the scenes but nonetheless proved pivotal. Aquinas was an adherent of intellectualism, a school of thought that elevated God's intellect over and above his will. By giving priority to the divine intellect, Aquinas avoided the charge that God's free will was arbitrary. Applied to justification, intellectualism meant that God would see the inherent value of one's merit and would be obligated to then respond with the just reward.

On the other hand, others, like William of Ockham (c. 1285-1347), the Oxford educated English Franciscan, advocated a very different scheme. Rather than embracing intellectualism, Ockham turned to voluntarism, which prioritised the divine will over the divine intellect. Ockham criticised Aquinas' intellectualism, arguing that it significantly restricted God's free will, obligating him to reward based on the inherent value of merit. In reality, Ockham argued, God can bestow his favour however he pleases.

The voluntarist approach was adopted by a later theologian in Germany by the name of Gabriel Biel (c. 1420-1495). Biel is often called the "last of the scholastics," arriving just on the eve of the Reformation. Though Biel would earn degrees from universities like Heidelberg, he did not limit himself to academic life, but was a priest and a preacher who, much like Pelagius, had an enormous concern for the practical piety of the common Christian. Biel was influenced by Ockham and in the century to come Biel would have considerable sway on Johann Eck, Luther's infamous opponent, as well as the Council of Trent (1545-63), which condemned Reformation doctrines like *sola fide* (faith alone). But more to the point, Biel represented, along with others before him such as Ockham and Robert Holcot (c. 1290-1349), the scholastic school of thought known as the *via moderna* (the modern way).

Like Ockham, Biel applied voluntarism to justification, concluding that God is free to reward however he sees fit. Cleverly, Biel combined voluntarism with the biblical concept of a divine covenant. According to Biel, God voluntarily chooses to make a covenant in which he promises to justify whoever does his best. If man does his best, infused grace will follow. To be clear, prior to the covenant God is in no way bound but is totally free. Even so, once he voluntarily binds himself to this covenant, he now obligates himself to reward anyone who does his best with justifying grace.

The covenant, he argued, is like the relationship between a King and his people. The King (God) has decided that he will accept his people if they fulfil the conditions of his covenant. What are these conditions? Man must do his best and, when he does, God will accept his deeds as sufficient for justification, even though such deeds are not inherently worthy. This concept was communicated in the popular motto: "God will not deny grace to anyone who does what lies within them." Though his best deeds are not perfect, God will accept them, much like a king would accept a lead coin as if it were a gold coin.

According to Biel, most of the resources one needs to do one's best and be justified lie within. For Biel, sin has not so damaged humanity that it is impossible for us to do good works apart from grace. The will is still capable of meritorious obedience. And when we do our best, God then rewards our

thomas aquinas

gabriel biel

c. 1420-1495

martin luther

natural effort by infusing grace within us. As Biel himself says in his sermon "Circumcision of the Lord": "Thus God has established the rule [covenant] that *whoever turns to Him and does what he can* will receive forgiveness of sins from God. God *infuses assisting grace* into such a man, who is thus taken back into friendship." Apart from the concept of covenant, Biel can sound Pelagian (God rewards those who do their best). Yet when our works are preceded by a covenant where God promises reward, suddenly God sounds very gracious.

In short, the *via moderna* of the fourteenth and fifteenth centuries did have a very optimistic view of human capacity for good, believing we could do what was necessary to attain a right relationship with God. Still, they denied that they were Pelagians reincarnated. The charge of Pelagianism, however, could not be avoided. Steven Ozment, in his book *The Age of Reform, 1250-1550*, explains:

Gabriel Biel, "The Circumcision of the Lord," in Heiko Oberman, *Forerunners of the Reformation: The Shape of Late Medieval Thought Illustrated by Key Documents* (Philadelphia: Fortress, 1966), 173. Emphasis added.

> In opposition to [Aquinas and company] making salvation *conditional* upon the presence of a *supernatural habit of grace*, Ockham argued that one could perform works acceptable to God simply *by doing the best one could with one's natural moral ability*. Not only did Ockham believe it possible for those lacking such a habit to love God above all things and detest sin, but he argued further that God found it "fitting" to *reward with an infusion of grace* those who did so. Whereas Aquinas… had required the presence of such grace before any positive relationship with God could exist, Ockham [and Biel] made the reception of grace a reward for *prior moral effort*. …Ockham appeared to free divine acceptance from absolute dependence on infused habits of grace only to make God's will dependent on the good works man could do in his natural moral state. Unassisted ethical cooperation now preceded, as a condition, the infusion of grace, which, with subsequent ethical cooperation, won man salvation. To the traditional mind such an argument was Pelagianism.

Steven Ozment, *The Age of Reform, 1250-1550: An Intellectual and Religious History of Late Medieval and Reformation Europe* (New Haven: Yale University Press, 1980), 41-42. Emphasis added.

pelagius   john   augustine
                  cassian

For these reasons, many opponents believed the *via moderna* was terribly unbiblical, convinced the charge of Pelagianism was valid, or Semi-Pelagianism at the very least. For example, the modern Augustinian school (*schola Augustiniana moderna*), represented by Thomas Bradwardine (author of *The Case of God against Pelagius*) and Gregory of Rimini (c. 1300-1358), argued for a return to Augustine, advocating for a pessimistic view of man's abilities.

Moreover, the modern Augustinian school believed that the *via moderna* created enormous pastoral problems. Applied to the Christian life, the *via moderna*'s understanding of justification – despite its best intentions – did not result in tremendous assurance of salvation. What, after all, would keep God from removing his justifying grace given the *via moderna*'s commitment to voluntarism? Lutheran theologian Korey Maas brings out this tension precisely:

> *Thus, at least in theory, God could justify sinners even without the bestowal of his grace and their subsequent cooperation. Further, and more worryingly, the opposite was also understood to be the case: being bound by no necessity, God might deny salvation even to those who cooperate with the grace he has provided. Ockham's reasoning, following that of his predecessor Duns Scotus, was that "nothing created must, for reasons intrinsic to it, be accepted by God." That is, neither grace nor one's cooperation with it are deserving of salvation in and of themselves; they are accepted and rewarded only because God has voluntarily agreed to do so. Ultimately, then, one's salvation was understood to be dependent not only upon divine grace together with human cooperation but also, and most fundamentally, upon God's keeping his promise to regard these as meriting eternal life.*

Korey D. Maas, "Justification by Faith Alone," in *Reformation Theology: A Systematic Summary*, ed. Matthew Barrett (Wheaton, IL: Crossway, 2017), 516.

The type of anxiety the *via moderna* created would be found not many years later in a German monk nearly driven to absolute despair as he relentlessly but unsuccessfully tried to live out Biel's justification doctrine on a daily basis. His name was Martin Luther.

thomas aquinas

gabriel biel

martin luther
1483-1546

The reformation of justification:
Martin Luther

Most turn to the famous 95 Theses to begin the story of the Reformation. Yet in light of the *via moderna*, it makes much more sense to start with Luther's early training, some of his first lectures on the Bible, and an early disputation that proved instrumental.

It's absolutely critical to keep in mind that Luther, by his own admission, did not decide on his theology of justification instantaneously. For Luther, there was development in his doctrine of justification. He received his doctorate in 1512 at the recently established University of Wittenberg (founded 1502). And it was at Wittenberg that Luther would become a lecturer as well, teaching on Psalms (1513-1515), Romans (1515-1516), Galatians (1516-1517), and Hebrews (1517-1518).

But bear in mind that when Luther started lecturing he did so with all the theological assumptions inherited from his training in medieval theology, particularly the *via moderna* school of thought. In fact, one of Luther's professors was John Nathin. In 1472 Nathin had committed himself to the Augustinians. Historians believe that Nathin studied under Biel at Tübingen for his doctoral studies and most likely heard Biel's lectures, specifically Biel's commentary on the canon of the mass. Nathin grew to love Biel, so he assigned Biel's commentary to Luther. It isn't surprising, then, that when Luther started lecturing on the Psalms he agreed with the theology of Gabriel Biel. "The teachers correctly say that to a man who does what is in him God gives grace without fail." Justification, for Luther, was not a forensic declaration based on grace alone through faith alone, but a progressive process of inward change and moral renewal until one is made righteous.

For a more extensive discussion of Nathin, Biel, and Luther, see Scott H. Hendrix, *Martin Luther: Visionary Reformer* (New Haven: Yale University Press, 2015), 36.

Martin Luther, *First Lectures on the Psalms II*, in *LW* 11:396.

Maas, "Justification by Faith Alone," 517-18.

Yet Luther's opinion would change. Luther started to evaluate Biel only to conclude that while he agreed with Biel on a variety of doctrinal subjects, he could no longer agree with him on that one subject that mattered most (i.e. the nature of grace, faith, and love). Between 1515-1516 Luther would begin to shift, though only just slightly. The years 1515-1516 represent Luther's lectures on Romans where he starts to reject the *via moderna* account of salvation. Instead of doing what lies within, we are passive as we embrace and experience divine grace, said Luther.

Maas, "Justification by Faith Alone," 517-18.

This rejection of the *via moderna*, and Biel in particular, became explicit in the year 1517. Luther prepared a set of theses for Franz Günther to defend at the University of Wittenberg, theses that have been titled *Disputation Against Scholastic Theology*. Foreshadowing Luther's future work, *The Bondage of the Will* (1525), these theses unapologetically argue that man is a "bad tree" and "can only will and do evil." It "is false to state that man's inclination is free to choose between either of two opposites. Indeed, the inclination is not free, but captive."

Martin Luther, *Disputation Against Scholastic Theology*, 1517, in *LW* 31:9 (theses 4, 5).

In the next thesis it becomes very clear who Luther is aiming for: "It is false to state that the will can by nature conform to correct precept. This is said in opposition to Scotus and Gabriel." Luther continues this line of thought in the rest of the disputation. The will, he argues, is "innately and inevitably evil and corrupt" and "is not free to strive toward whatever is declared good. ...in opposition to Scotus and Gabriel." Then comes one of Luther's most profound statements: "Man is by nature unable to want God to be God. Indeed, he himself wants to be God, and does not want God to be God."

Luther, *Disputation Against* (thesis 6).

Luther, *Disputation Against* (thesis 9).

Luther, *Disputation Against* (thesis 17). Luther then denies Biel the right to apply his voluntarism to justification: The grace of God cannot happen "through the absolute power of God" as if "an act of friendship may be present without the presence of the grace of God" and this "in opposition to Gabriel." Of course, Luther recognises that Biel's voluntarism in justification is but the product of Ockham, for he writes next that it "is not true that God can accept man without his justifying grace" and this "in opposition to Ockham." Similar theological emphases would reappear in the immediate aftermath of Luther's 95 Theses, as seen in the theses he prepared for the Heidelberg Disputation, which proved instrumental for onlookers, like Martin Bucer, as they transitioned out of Rome and into the Reformation fold. Luther, *Disputation Against* (theses 55, 56).

thomas
aquinas

gabriel
biel

martin
luther
1483-1546

Nonetheless, in these early years Luther had yet to arrive at his permanent understanding of justification. Luther had simply transitioned out of the *via moderna* into the more Augustinian understanding of grace described earlier. No doubt, this was a giant step, one that should not be undervalued. Yet Luther still assumed justification to be a progressive process of moral, ontological change, not necessarily a forensic declaration, though Luther, as an Augustinian, would credit God's grace with the change that takes place within. On the one hand, Luther now understood, thanks to Augustine, that Scripture says the ungodly are justified by the righteousness of God. On the other hand, justification still meant being made inherently righteous. A gracious substance had to be infused, one that would heal the individual and make him well again. This meant, then, that the Christian was only partly righteous; his other part was sinful. Justification, for the early Luther, may have been God initiated and due to God's grace alone, but it still incorporated a process of being made godly. Luther says it this way in his lectures on Romans: "God has not yet justified us, that is, he has not made us perfectly righteous or declared our righteousness perfect, but he has made a beginning in order that he might make us perfect."

Maas, "Justification by Faith Alone," 518-19.

LW 25:245.

All that would change the closer Luther came to 1520/1521. As Lutheran theologian Korey Maas has observed, rather than describing justification as involving a healing righteousness (an imparted or infused substance; an inherent trait), Luther begins to describe grace, as seen in his work *Against Latomus*, in terms of the "favour of God." Why the sudden change? Maas persuasively demonstrates that Luther's theological adjustment was due, at least in part, to the influence of Philip Melanchthon, who was hired on faculty at Wittenberg in 1518. In 1520, for example, Melanchthon starts to refer to grace as "God's favour." In his 1521 *Loci Communes* Melanchthon would argue that the "word 'grace' does not mean some quality in us, but rather the very will of God, or the goodwill of God toward us." Justification was not something to be attained in the future based upon progressive moral renewal in the present. Instead, justification and righteousness was a present reality concerning one's new status. Since grace was not an infused quality or substance but was instead God's favour, the believer's justification was no longer something he hoped to one day achieve but was something God had given to him here and now.

Maas, "Justification by Faith Alone," 520-521.

Philipp Melanchthon, *Loci Communes Theologici* (1521), in *Melanchthon and Bucer*, ed. Wilhelm Pauck, trans. Lowell J. Satre, LCC 19 (Philadelphia: Westminster, 1969), 87.

Maas, "Justification by Faith Alone," 521-522.

Luther's new understanding of justification became explicit in 1519, 1520, and 1521, particularly in works like *Two Kinds of Righteousness* and *The Freedom of a Christian*. And as the decades wore on, Luther only further solidified his view, most brilliantly displayed, for example, in his 1535 *Lectures on Galatians*. He still spoke of the Christian being simultaneously righteous and a sinner, but now it meant something very different: the believer was already declared righteous in status despite continuing to sin in their life. Righteousness no longer referred to an inward moral quality but to an external, alien status that one received by faith alone. This righteous status is imputed to the one who trusts in Christ. And the righteousness imputed is none other than the righteousness of Christ. Whereas we failed to uphold the law, Christ has, as our representative, obeyed the law perfectly and his impeccable record of obedience is then reckoned to us as a gift. In other words, not only has Christ removed the penalty of the law against our sin by means of his substitutionary death on the cross, but he has also fulfilled that very law in our place. The result? We do not merely have our sins removed but his righteousness added to our account, giving us the righteous status we need to stand before God and enter into his eternal life.

In terms of assurance of salvation, Luther believed he succeeded where Biel failed. The imputed, alien righteousness of Christ proved to be the Christian's weapon against the devil's attack on our conscience. The "afflicted conscience," Luther advised, "has no remedy against despair and eternal death except to take hold of the promise of grace offered in Christ, that is, this righteousness of faith, this passive or Christian righteousness." Rather than trusting in one's own righteousness through the Law (what Luther labelled "active righteousness"), one should instead look to "passive righteousness," that is, the righteousness of Jesus. "Thus I put myself beyond all active righteousness, all righteousness of my own or of the divine Law, and I embrace only that passive righteousness which is the righteousness of grace, mercy, and the forgiveness of sins." The righteousness of Christ, says Luther, is not a righteousness we "perform but receive," it is not one we "have but accept, when God the Father grants it to us through Jesus Christ."

Maas helpfully captures this point: "Most revealing of this new emphasis was the radical repurposing of that concept of which he had made use already in his earlier Romans lectures, that of the Christian being righteous and sinful at the same time. No longer did this formula express the idea that one was partly sinful and partly righteous, or a present sinner with the future hope of being made righteous; the Christian now remained in himself completely a sinner yet, by means of faith and in the eyes of God, completely righteous." Maas, "Justification by faith alone," 522.

The quotes in this paragraph are all taken from Luther's introduction to his lectures on Galatians. *LW* 26:5-6.

thomas aquinas

gabriel biel

martin luther
1483-1546

Luther's final warning

How important was Luther's breakthrough to the Reformation cause? Very! For Luther, it not only was the dividing line – along with *sola scriptura* – with Roman Catholicism, but it was the source of life for any reformation that was to follow. As Luther said at the start of his *Lectures on Galatians*:

> *There is a clear and present danger that the devil may take away from us the pure doctrine of faith and may substitute for it the doctrines of works and of human traditions. It is very necessary, therefore, that this doctrine of faith be continually read and heard in public. ...this doctrine can never be discussed and taught enough. If it is lost and perishes, the whole knowledge of truth, life, and salvation is lost and perishes at the same time. But if it flourishes, everything good flourishes – religion, true worship, the glory of God, and the right knowledge of all things and of all social conditions.*

LW 26:3.

This year, 2017, is the 500th anniversary of the Reformation. What would Luther say to us Protestants today? In the light of many contemporary challenges to the Reformation doctrine of justification by grace alone through faith alone in Christ alone, certainly Luther would leave us with a warning:

> **"If the doctrine of justification is lost, the whole Christian doctrine is lost."** LW 26:9.

An excerpt from the works of John Owen with an introduction and annotations by Paul Gibson.

The Only Refuge of Distressed Consciences

introduction

Following Luther's Reformation breakthrough on justification, debates within Protestantism continued into the seventeenth century. These were no mere academic disputes. The pastor-theologian John Owen (1616-83) saw this clearly. He commented that, though many different views of justification were held, all agreed that understanding it rightly is "of the highest importance to the souls of men." Owen knew that unbiblical accounts of justification would have serious pastoral consequences for the consciences and for the very souls of men and women. Getting it right mattered.

John Owen, *The Doctrine of Justification by Faith through the Imputation of the Righteousness of Christ Explained, Confirmed, and Vindicated* (1677; p1-400 in vol. 5 of *The Works of John Owen*; repr. Banner of Truth, 1967), 3.

The seventeenth century was a time of substantial political upheaval, including the English Civil War and the Commonwealth under Oliver Cromwell. At different times during the century, different groups enjoyed more theological popularity and influence. Owen wrote extensively on justification, often to defend the biblical gospel against opposing views, whether from the Roman Catholics, the Socinians, or fellow-Protestants such as Richard Baxter (well-known to many as the author of *The Reformed Pastor*).

Socinianism was a theological system, named after Faustus Socinus, which rejected the deity of Christ.

Owen's fullest treatment of justification was his 1677 book, *The Doctrine of Justification by Faith*. Here he interacts with opposing views, biblically and theologically defending justification by faith alone. Owen begins by emphasising the vital pastoral importance of this doctrine. He is concerned with "the proper relief of the conscience of a sinner pressed and perplexed with a sense of the guilt of sin." Before we can grasp the truth about justification, we must have a right sense of the holiness of God and the sinfulness of our sin. Then, in the first eight chapters, Owen addresses the nature of justifying faith, the role of faith in justification, the full completion of justification at the moment of conversion, the imputation of Christ's righteousness to the believer, and the imputation of the believer's sin to Christ.

Owen, *Doctrine of Justification*, 7.

Owen, *Doctrine of Justification*, 13-24.

The word 'impute' means to credit or count something to an account, as in our sin being placed in Jesus' account, and his righteousness being credited to us, counted as ours, as if we had performed it.

The following extract is taken from chapter 9, where Owen circles around the question "What is the righteousness by which we are justified before God?" Owen's prose can feel very hard work, and he comes at this question from several angles, but he is well worth the effort as he helps us think through the nature of Christ's imputed righteousness, the role of union with Christ, the relation of justification to the certainty of eternal life, and the pastoral consequences for the souls of men and women.

Owen, *Doctrine of Justification*, 205-209.

EXTRACT: John Owen, *The Doctrine of Justification by Faith through the Imputation of the Righteousness of Christ Explained, Confirmed, and Vindicated* (1677; p1-400 in vol. 5 of *The Works of John Owen*; repr. Banner of Truth, 1967). The text reproduced here is an adapted and slightly modernised version of Goold's 19th century edition.

chapter 9.
The Nature, Cause, and Instrument of Justification

The principal differences about the doctrine of justification are reducible to three topics: the nature of justification, the cause of justification, and its instrument; that is, what is required of us.

1. the nature of justification

That is, a legal courtroom verdict in which God declares the person righteous.

This phrase indicates that, for Owen, the believer's justification gives her the right to inherit eternal life. This contrasts with the views of many of his opponents, including the Roman Catholics, the Socinians, and Baxter, who spoke in terms of two justifications: an initial justification by faith, followed by a progressive or final justification based at least partly on works. Some modern theologians have argued for a similar position. Instead, Owen wants to emphasise that, the moment she first believes, the believer is fully justified before God (there is no second justification) and is therefore certain of eternal life – the final verdict has already been declared, by faith alone.

Here we consider the nature of justification, namely, whether it consists of an internal change of the person justified, by the imputation of a habit of inherent grace or righteousness; or whether it be a forensic act, in the judging, esteeming, declaring, and pronouncing such a person to be righteous, thereby absolving him from all his sins, giving him the right and title to life. Here we have to do only with those of the Church of Rome, because all others, both Protestants and Socinians, are agreed on the forensic sense of the word, and the nature of the thing signified by it. And this I have already addressed, so far as our present task requires; and that, I hope, with such evidence of truth as cannot easily be disputed.

In this opening paragraph Owen explains the first of three main differences between competing views of justification: namely, the nature of justification. The question is, does the word 'justification' in the Bible refer to an internal change in the believer, or a legal (forensic) declaration in God's courtroom? The Roman Catholic Church understands 'justification' to be about internal change (God giving the believer a habit of inherent grace or righteousness). Protestants, in contrast, understand 'justification' to be a one-off legal verdict at the moment of conversion. Earlier, in chapter 4, Owen has examined the Hebrew and Greek words that we translate 'justify' and shown from Scripture that the word refers to a legal verdict.

Nor may it be supposed that we have insisted too long upon this, as an opinion which is obsolete, and long since sufficiently refuted. I think much otherwise, and that those who avoid these controversies with the Romanists will give a greater appearance of fear than of contempt; for when all is done, if *free justification through the blood of Christ*, and the imputation of his righteousness, be not able to preserve its place in the minds of men, then the Popish doctrine of justification must and will return upon the world, with all that accompanies and flows from it.

Like 'Papist', which Owen will use later, 'Romanist' is a term for a member or supporter of the Roman Catholic Church.

Whilst any knowledge of the law or gospel is continued amongst us, the consciences of men will at one time or other, living or dying, be deeply affected with a sense of sin, with regard to its guilt and danger. Hence that trouble and those anxieties of mind will ensue, as will force men, be they never so unwilling, to seek after some relief and satisfaction. And what will not men attempt who are reduced to the condition expressed, (Micah 6:6-7)?

When Owen refers to the law and the gospel, in common with many of his contemporaries, he uses 'law' to mean the commands of Scripture (in both Testaments), and 'gospel' to mean the Bible's promises of free salvation through Christ.

Micah 6:6-7
With what shall I come before the LORD
and bow down before the exalted God?
Shall I come before him with burnt offerings,
with calves a year old?
Will the LORD be pleased with thousands of rams,
with ten thousand rivers of oil?
Shall I offer my firstborn for my transgression,
the fruit of my body for the sin of my soul?

Therefore, in this case, if the *true and only relief* of distressed consciences of sinners who are weary and heavy-laden be hid from their eyes, – if they have no understanding of, nor trust in, that which alone they may set against the sentence of the law, and place between God's justice and their souls, in which they may take shelter from the storms of that wrath which abides on those that do not believe, – they will take to themselves anything which confidently promises them present ease and relief.

Hence many persons, living all their days in an ignorance of the righteousness of God, are oftentimes on their sick-beds, and in their dying hours, converted to a confidence in the ways of rest and peace which the Romanists impose upon them; for such seasons of advantage do they wait for, to advance the reputation, as they suppose, of their own zeal, – but in truth they bring scandal to the Christian religion. But finding at any time the consciences of men under anxiety, and ignorant of or disbelieving that heavenly relief which is provided in the gospel, they are ready with their applications and medicines, claiming the approval of history, and an innumerable company of devout souls with them.

Such is their doctrine of justification, with the addition of those other ingredients of confession, absolution, penances, or commutations, aids from saints and angels, especially the blessed Virgin; all warmed by the fire of purgatory, and confidently administered to persons sick of ignorance, darkness, and sin. And let none please themselves in the contempt of these things. If the truth concerning justification be once disbelieved among us, or obliterated by any strategies emerging from the minds of men, then at one time or other, they must and will seek rest and peace in these things.

The commuting or reduction of a punishment for sin.

As for the new schemes and projections of justification, which some at present would supply us with, they are no way suited nor able to give relief or satisfaction to a conscience really troubled by sin, and seriously inquiring how it may have rest and peace with God. I shall be bold, therefore, whoever be offended at it, to say that *if we lose the ancient doctrine of justification through faith in the blood of Christ*, and the imputation of his righteousness to us, then the public confession of religion will quickly issue in *Popery* or *Atheism*, or at least in what is the next door to it.

In this paragraph Owen emphasises the vital pastoral importance of justification by faith alone. Owen takes his stand on "free justification through the blood of Christ, and the imputation of his righteousness." If this is lost, the result will be a return to the Roman Catholic position. For Owen, this is not merely theologically disastrous; it is also pastorally devastating. In life, and especially when facing death, the believer considers God's law, God's holy character, and his own sinfulness, and his conscience is distressed. What he needs is "that heavenly relief which is provided in the gospel," that is, the comfort of free justification by faith alone. Those, such as the Roman Catholic Church, who are "ignorant of or disbelieving" this doctrine, cannot minister that desperately needed comfort. Owen says they are "no way suited nor able to give relief or satisfaction to a conscience really troubled for sin."

2. the formal cause of justification

Owen now turns to the second main difference between competing views of justification. The language of 'formal cause' is drawn from the Greek philosopher Aristotle, and was commonly used in seventeenth century debates on justification. Even Owen thinks these terms aren't that important and too easily produce a "strife of words"! He's more interested in something else: Having argued that justification is a legal verdict, he now asks 'How it is that that verdict is passed?' 'Is it because of our own merit, or the "satisfaction and merit of Christ"?'

The second principal controversy is about the *formal cause* of justification, as it is expressed and stated by those of the Roman Church; and under these terms some Protestant theologians have consented to debate the matter in difference. I shall not enter into a strife of words; – so the Romanists will call that which we inquire after. Some of ours say the righteousness of Christ imputed, some, the imputation of the righteousness of Christ, is the formal cause of our justification; some, that there is no formal cause of justification, but this is that which supplies the place and use of a formal cause, which is the righteousness of Christ. In none of these things will I concern myself, though I judge what was mentioned in the last place to be most proper and significant.

The substance of the inquiry with which we are concerned is, *What is that righteousness whereby and wherewith a believing sinner is justified before God*; or whereon he is accepted with God, has his sins pardoned, is received into grace and favour, and has a title given him to the heavenly inheritance? I shall propose this inquiry, knowing that it contains the substance of what convinced sinners do look after in and by the gospel.

It is agreed by all, except the Socinians, that the *primary* or *procuring* cause of the pardon of our sins and acceptance with God is the satisfaction and merit of Christ.

However, it cannot be denied that some, retaining the names of them, do seem to renounce or disbelieve the things themselves; but we need not to take any notice of this, until they are free more plainly to express their minds. But as concerning the righteousness itself inquired after, there seems to be a difference among them who yet all deny it to be the righteousness of Christ imputed to us.

For those of the Roman Church plainly say that, upon the infusion of a habit of grace, with the expulsion of sin, and the renovation of our natures thereby (which they call the first justification) we are actually justified before God by our own works of righteousness. Hereon they dispute about the merit and satisfactoriness of those works, with their entitlement to the reward of eternal life.

Others, such as the Socinians, *openly disclaim all merit* in our works; only some, out of reverence, as I suppose, to the antiquity of the word, and under the shelter of the ambiguity of its signification, have faintly attempted an accommodation with it. But in the substance of what they assert, to the best of my understanding, they are all agreed: for what the Papists call "justitia operum," – the righteousness of works, – they call a personal, inherent, evangelical righteousness; of which we have spoken before. And whereas the Papists say that this righteousness of works is not absolutely perfect, nor in itself able to justify us in the sight of God, but owes all its worth and dignity to the merit of Christ, they affirm that this evangelical righteousness is the condition whereby we enjoy the benefits of the righteousness of Christ, in the pardon of our sins, and the acceptance of our persons before God.

However, to those who will acknowledge *no other righteousness* by which we are justified before God, the meaning is the same, whether we say that *on the condition of this righteousness* we are made partakers of the benefits of the righteousness of Christ, or that *it is the righteousness of Christ* which makes this righteousness of ours accepted with God. But these things must afterwards more particularly be inquired into.

> In this paragraph Owen makes some fine but important distinctions. Aside from the Socinians, all sides agree that Christ's satisfaction and merit (his atoning sacrifice and perfect righteousness) are essential for the believer to be justified. The question becomes: Is Christ's satisfaction and merit **alone** the righteousness on the basis of which believers are justified? Owen explains that Roman Catholics speak of 'the righteousness of works', while others (such as Baxter) speak of 'personal, inherent, evangelical righteousness'; in both cases such good works are part of the basis for justification, alongside Christ's righteousness. As such both reject justification by faith **alone**; both teach that the righteousness by which we are justified is Christ's righteousness plus the Christian's own obedience, which for Owen is a catastrophic error.

3. what is required of us?

The third inquiry about which there is no agreement in this matter is what is required on our part – upon the assumption of a necessity that he who is to be justified should, one way or other, be interested in the righteousness of Christ. This some say to be faith alone; others, faith and works also, and that in the same kind of necessity and use. The view we presently challenge is the second one proposed; and, indeed, herein lies the substance of the whole controversy about our justification before God; upon the determination and the stating of this depends the answer to all other related questions.

What follows is Owen's answer to the big question in this whole chapter: what is the righteousness on the basis of which the believer is justified?

This, therefore, is that which I affirm: *The righteousness of Christ (in his obedience and suffering for us) imputed to believers, as they are united to him by his Spirit, is that righteousness by which they are justified before God, on account of which their sins are pardoned, and a right is granted them to the heavenly inheritance.*

Here Owen hints at a distinction he develops in much more detail in chapter 12: Christ's righteousness involves both active and passive obedience. Christ's active obedience refers to his positive obedience to all the law's commands (here 'in his obedience'). His passive obedience refers to his suffering the law's penalty for sin in our place (here 'and suffering for us'), as in the word 'passion' (suffering). Owen will go on to argue that the believer needs both Christ's active and his passive obedience imputed to him. That is, if Christ suffered for our sins but did not also credit to us his perfect positive obedience to the law, then we are left still needing to obey the law ourselves to be justified. This is pastorally vital, because it takes away the fear that we might have to add our own good deeds to be accepted by God: we are already clothed with the righteousness (perfect obedience) of Christ; how could anything we do ever improve on what we already have? Or, to put it another way, our justification means not merely that God sees us 'just as if I'd never sinned', but more than that, he sees us 'just as if I'd always perfectly obeyed': Owen's point is that nothing - no works of ours – can or need be added.

The connection Owen makes between union and imputation is striking in light of more recent views on justification. Some recent writers, such as N. T. Wright and Rich Lusk, have argued that union with Christ makes imputation unnecessary [N. T. Wright, Justification: God's Plan and Paul's Vision (London: SPCK, 2009), 205; Rich Lusk, "A Response to 'The Biblical Plan of Salvation'," in The Auburn Avenue Theology Pros & Cons: Debating the Federal Vision *(ed. E. Calvin Beisner; Fort Lauderdale: Knox Theological Seminary, 2004), 141-43]. In contrast, for Owen, union is the very basis for imputation. Christ and the believer are not two separate persons, with righteousness as a substance passed from one side of God's courtroom to another, as this doctrine has sometimes been caricatured. Christ and the believer are united as one person, such that what the head accomplishes, he accomplishes for the body too.*

This position plainly and fully expresses the substance of that doctrine, in this important article of evangelical truth for which we plead. And I have chosen to express it thus, because it is that thesis wherein the learned Davenant laid down that common doctrine of the Reformed churches whose defence he undertook. This is the shield of truth in the whole cause of justification; which, whilst it is preserved safe, we need not trouble ourselves about the differences that are among learned men about the most proper stating and declaration of some lesser details of it. This is the refuge, the only refuge, of distressed consciences, wherein they may find rest and peace.

John Davenant, Bishop of Salisbury 1621-1641.

if you liked this...

...or want something a little easier, try:

1. **Robert Traill, *Justification Vindicated* (1692; repr. Edinburgh: Banner of Truth, 2002).** Much shorter and easier to read than Owen, Traill defends the Protestant doctrine of justification by faith alone, responding to the unorthodox views of opponents such as Baxter, and showing why a right understanding of this doctrine is so important.

2. **Thomas Goodwin, *Christ Set Forth as the Cause of Justification and as the Source of Justification* (1642; repr. Edinburgh: Banner of Truth, 2015).** Goodwin was a contemporary of Owen and a fellow Congregational pastor. This book is both readable and full of pastoral application, expounding Romans 8:34 and encouraging Christians to look to Christ and not to themselves for their assurance.

3. **John Owen, *The Doctrine of Justification by Faith, Through the Imputation of the Righteousness of Christ; Explained, Confirmed, and Vindicated* (1677; p1-400 in vol. 5 of *The Works of John Owen*; repr. Edinburgh: Banner of Truth, 1967).** This is the book from which our excerpt was taken. Although Owen takes more time and effort to read than the above two titles, it is time and effort well spent. Owen's biblical and systematic exposition of the doctrine is thorough and masterly.

4. **Martin Luther, *The Freedom of a Christian* (1520; repr. Minneapolis, MN: Fortress, 2008).** This short work by Luther is very readable and is a good starting point for understanding Luther's insights on justification.

5. **John Calvin and Jacopo Sadoleto, *A Reformation Debate* (ed. John C. Olin; New York: Fordham University Press, 2000).** This correspondence between the Protestant Calvin and the Roman Catholic Sadoleto brings out clearly the serious differences between the Roman Catholic and the Reformation doctrines of justification. Another place to read Calvin on justification is in his *Institutes*, Book 3, chapters 11-18. ▶

a justified divide

Protestants and Catholics on the doctrine of justification
by Gregg R. Allison

Some of the following discussion is taken from Chris Castaldo and Gregg Allison, "The Pope Offers Mercy – Protestants Won't Be Indulged," The Gospel Coalition, September 13, 2016.

The Roman Catholic Church celebrated 2016 as the Year of Mercy. At the heart of this special Jubilee Year was the granting of indulgences for the purpose of removing the punishment for the sins of the Catholic faithful. Specifically,

> An indulgence is a remission before God of the temporal punishment due to sins whose guilt has already been forgiven, which the faithful Christian who is duly disposed gains under certain prescribed conditions through the action of the Church which, as the minister of redemption, dispenses and applies with authority the treasury of the satisfactions of Christ and the saints.

Catechism of the Catholic Church, 1471

Throughout this article, 'Church' refers to the Roman Catholic church when capitalised.

The Sale of Indulgences

In medieval theology, like today, the sacrament of penance required repentant sinners to make satisfaction for their transgressions through works of mercy. This involved saying prayers, serving the poor, giving alms, or going on a pilgrimage. In the year 1095, Pope Urban II decreed that penitents would be released from their obligation to perform these works if they joined the crusade against the Turks. Subsequent popes repeated this provision by offering indulgences on other occasions. In gratitude, the faithful offered financial gifts to the Church.

The custom of transacting indulgences escalated and eventually grew into a significant revenue stream. An inflexion point occurred in 1476 when Pope Sixtus IV issued *Salvator Noster*, extending penitential satisfaction to deceased individuals for whom an indulgence was offered. So, for example, when Martin Luther visited Rome in 1510-11 and climbed Pilate's stairway on his knees - the *scala sancta*, praying on each step - he did so on behalf of his grandfather. Such devotion was commonplace.

The indulgence trade came to a head after Pope Julius II issued a "Jubilee Indulgence" in 1507 to support the construction of the new St. Peter's Basilica in Rome. Urgency to fund the building project set in motion indulgence preachers who travelled through Europe. The Protestant Reformation began very largely as a protest against this practice, and the rest, as they say, is history. Catholic reform eventually abolished the sale of indulgences, but the custom of granting them continues to the present, as illustrated by Pope Francis's Extraordinary Jubilee Year of Mercy.

Adapted from Castaldo and Allison, "The Pope Offers Mercy - Protestants Won't Be Indulged."

Whereas there are various ways for the Catholic faithful to secure indulgences, the Church provided a global means during the Year of Mercy: it opened a Holy Door of Mercy in every Catholic cathedral (for example, St. Peter's Basilica in Rome) and at major pilgrimage sites (for example, the Sanctuary of Lourdes in France) throughout the world. And whereas there are two types of indulgences – providing either a partial or a plenary (complete) remission of all temporal punishment due to sin – the Church established the type of indulgence that would be obtained by passing through a Holy Door to be a plenary indulgence.

Evangelicals tend to dismissively laugh at this method of obtaining divine mercy. Even more, they may be appalled at the idea: how could and why would God grant mercy to people just because they walk through a particular door in a particular church or religious site? Before jumping to such an evaluation, evangelicals need to realise the process of obtaining mercy through a plenary indulgence is more extensive than taking a stroll through an entryway. Four prerequisites must be satisfied first (the following are the instructions found at the entrance to the Holy Door of the Basilica della Madonna di San Luca, Bologna, Italy):

My translation.

(1) pray (the Creed, the Our Father, the Hail Mary, the Gloria…) and [pray] for the needs of the Holy Father; (2) within fifteen days, approach the sacrament of Penance, confessing one's sins, and participate in the Mass, taking Holy Communion; (3) have the inner attitude of actual and affective separation from every sin, not only grave and mortal, but also slight and venial; (4) engage in a work of mercy, whether corporeal or spiritual.

When faithful Catholics satisfy these prerequisites, they are in state of grace and thus can walk through a Holy Door. They obtain a plenary indulgence for themselves, thereby remitting the temporal punishment due to their sins. Should they die in this state of grace, they would immediately enter into heaven. Or they may secure a plenary indulgence for the sake of their deceased relatives or friends in purgatory, by which their suffering souls would enter into heaven. The indulgence lasts for the entire day, and it may be secured once a day.

Evangelicals gasp more disconcertedly: how could and why would God grant mercy to people just because they pray, participate in certain sacraments, distance themselves from sin, and do good works? Such an approach is the very one denied by Paul: "we know that a person is not justified by works of the law but through faith in Jesus Christ, so we also have believed in Christ Jesus, in order to be justified by faith in Christ and not by works of the law, because by works of the law no one will be justified" (Gal 2:16). If justification is by faith and not by rightly disposing oneself to divine grace and meeting certain prescribed conditions set by the Church, why this Catholic emphasis on indulgences and purgatory?

Much of the following discussion is adapted from Gregg R. Allison, Roman Catholic Theology and Practice: An Evangelical Assessment (Wheaton: Crossway, 2014), ch. 13.

This brings us to the heart of the matter: the continuing disagreement between the Roman Catholic and Protestant views of justification. In this year of the five hundredth anniversary of the Protestant Reformation, this doctrinal difference is still front and centre. We begin with a presentation of Catholic theology, followed by the traditional Protestant position.

The Roman Catholic Doctrine of Justification

See opposite page.

CCC 1989. The citation is taken from Canons and Decrees of the Council of Trent, 6th session (January 13, 1547), Decree on Justification, 7.

In accordance with the Council of Trent, the Roman Catholic Church defines justification as "not only the remission of sins, but also the sanctification and renewal of the interior man." Importantly, this Catholic position combines forgiveness of sins, sanctification, and regeneration. Clearly, justification is not a divine declaration, as it is according to Protestant theology, to which we will return. Moreover, this definition, as formulated by the Council of Trent, was originally intended to differentiate Catholic theology of justification from Protestant theology's position. As it was then, so it is now: the two traditions are still divided over justification. This continued divergence is confirmed by a more detailed look at the Catholic view.

The Council of Trent met in Northern Italy (in Trento and Bologna) between 1545-1563. It produced a number of decrees and canons which rejected and condemned the Protestant Reformation, and re-stated the Catholic position on issues of justification, Scripture, the sacraments, ministry and priesthood, marriage, and purgatory.

Justification, conversion and inward renewal

To start, Catholic theology affirms, "The first work of the grace of the Holy Spirit is conversion, effecting justification." That is, conversion precedes and leads to justification: "Moved by grace, man turns toward God and away from sin, thus accepting forgiveness and righteousness from on high."

CCC 1989. Cf. 1990: "Justification follows upon God's merciful initiative of offering forgiveness."

CCC 1989.

The decrees and condemnations of the Council of Trent continue as part of the Church's official teaching by the Second Vatican Council (1962-65) and the Catechism of the Catholic Church – the 'CCC' (1992).

Importantly, and perhaps surprisingly for Protestants, Catholic theology emphasises the initiating role of grace, underscoring "no one can merit the initial grace of forgiveness and justification."

CCC 2010.

Prompted by this grace, sinful people give their "free response," turning from sin and toward God. Such conversion effects their justification, which "is at the same time *the acceptance of God's righteousness* through faith in Jesus Christ," where righteousness is defined as "the rectitude of divine love." Moreover, justification conforms people "to the righteousness of God, who makes us inwardly just by the power of his mercy." Thus, justification focuses on transformation of people: their nature begins to become actually righteous, expressed in love for God and others.

CCC 2002.

CCC 1991. Emphasis original.

CCC 1992.

Justification by faith and baptism

Whereas Catholic and Protestant theology agree the atoning sacrifice of Jesus Christ is the ground of justification and the purpose of justification is God's glory and the gift of eternal life, the two diverge again in terms of how people appropriate justification. For Catholic theology, the appropriation is through faith and the sacrament of baptism: "Justification is conferred in Baptism, the sacrament of faith." As we will see, Protestant theology underscores justification is by faith alone.

CCC 1992.

Justification by co-operation

The divergence grows: Catholic theology maintains justification establishes cooperation between God and the Catholic faithful. On the divine side is the initiating and sustaining work of the grace of the Spirit. His action – known as 'illumination and inspiration' – incites and fosters the faithful's response. This human side of cooperation "is expressed by the assent of faith to the Word of God, which invites him to conversion, and in the cooperation of charity with the prompting of the Holy Spirit who precedes and preserves his assent." Again, in accordance with the Council of Trent, Catholic theology explains: "When God touches man's heart through the illumination of the Holy Spirit, man himself is not inactive while receiving that inspiration, since he could reject it; and yet, without God's grace, he cannot by his own free will move himself toward justice in God's sight." As the Holy Spirit acts graciously, the Catholic faithful, who could never initiate a move toward God and who could always resist such divine grace, instead freely cooperate with it: they convert, give the assent of faith, experience inwardly transforming righteousness, and work with love to love God and others. Again, the fusion of justification, regeneration, and sanctification is evident: "The Holy Spirit is the master of the interior life. By giving birth to the 'inner man,' justification entails the sanctification of his whole being."

Grace and the sacraments

Because Protestant theology often regards the Catholic view of salvation as being grace-less, it is important to underscore that justification is closely tied to grace; indeed, "justification comes from the grace of God." Grace is defined as "favor, the free and undeserved help that God gives us to respond to his call to become children of God, partakers of the divine nature and of eternal life." Importantly, though, grace is – indeed, must be – communicated through the sacraments of the Catholic Church. God has established an interdependent relationship between nature – created things

The Sacraments

Within Catholic theology there are seven sacraments, through which grace is received: baptism, confirmation, the Eucharist, penance, anointing of the sick, holy orders, matrimony.

By contrast, the Protestant Reformers argued that only two were instituted by Jesus: baptism and the Lord's Supper.

such as angels, mountains, plants, human beings, water, oil, bread, and wine – and his grace. Nature is capable of receiving and transmitting divine grace, and divine grace must be transmitted through the concrete elements of nature.

Thus, grace for justification is initiated by the sacrament of baptism, but grace itself "is the gratuitous gift that God makes to us of his own life, infused by the Holy Spirit into our soul to heal it of sin and to sanctify it." Moreover, grace for justification continues to be mediated through the other sacraments. For example, the sacrament of Confirmation completes baptismal grace, binding the baptised more closely to the Church and conferring upon them the special strength of the Spirit. For those who have fallen into mortal sin, the Church prescribes the sacrament of Penance by which it absolves them of their sin and restores to them justifying grace. Of course, the apex of the sacraments is the Eucharist, which provides grace that augments the faithful's union with Christ, separates them from sin, and more.

CCC 1999.

As already noted, the grace that is communicated through the seven sacraments is infused into the Catholic faithful, thereby transforming their nature, a process that endures throughout their lifetime. Indeed, grace operates by "giving birth to the inner man," effects "the sanctification of his whole being," and makes him "inwardly just." As we will see, this Catholic emphasis on the infusion of grace for ongoing inward renewal stands in stark contrast to the evangelical emphasis on the imputation of righteousness.

CCC 1995, 1992.

Grace and merit

Finally, through this grace, the Catholic faithful are enabled to earn merits and thus to gain eternal salvation. A merit is the recompense God owes to the faithful in terms of reward for their cooperation with his grace. As this notion sounds strange to Protestants, Catholic theology emphasises that "God has freely chosen to associate man with the work of his grace." Though the way of salvation could be different, God himself has established the process to be synergistic, that is, a divine and human cooperative effort. God initiates the process of justification through his provision of grace. This is followed by a free human response. As divinely-designed, this cooperation between God and people enables them to merit eternal life through their ongoing dependence on the sacraments, prayer, love, and good deeds. Importantly, Catholic theology emphasises "the merit of good works is to be attributed in the first place to the grace of God, then to the faithful." As already noted, such merit is not involved at the beginning of salvation; God alone initiates grace for salvation: "no one can merit the initial grace of forgiveness and justification, at the beginning of conversion." But when the faithful, prompted by the Holy Spirit and love, respond to divine grace, they merit for themselves and for others "the graces needed for [their] sanctification, for the increase of grace and charity, and for the attainment of eternal life."

CCC 2008.

CCC 2008.

CCC 2010.

CCC 2010.

The Protestant Doctrine of Justification

Protestant theology considers justification to be a legal pronouncement by which God declares a person "not guilty" but "righteous" instead. Such a divine speech-act is similar to the declaration a pastor makes at the end of a wedding ceremony when he voices these (or similar) words: "I now pronounce you husband and wife." His declaration makes it so; the man and the woman are now legally united in covenant relationship as husband and wife. So it is with justification: God's pronouncement makes it so. The ungodly person, declared to be "not guilty," is forgiven of all her sins. Additionally, declared to be "righteous," she stands before God as having fulfilled all the requirements of the law, not because she herself has fulfilled them, but because the righteousness of Jesus Christ has been credited to her account.

This evangelical doctrine of justification is first and foremost grounded in Scripture. The Bible uses the term "justification" in contrast with the term "condemnation" in legal discussions (e.g. Deut 25:1; Prov 17:15; Rom 5:16, 18). Condemnation is the divine verdict for the wicked, whereas justification is the opposite sentence. Remarkably (because it is all by divine grace), God "justifies the ungodly" (Rom 4:5). He does not forgive and declare righteous those who are working hard to secure his love, who are doing all they can to cooperate with his grace to merit eternal life. Quite the opposite: God "justifies the ungodly."

Paul underscores the legal, declarative nature of justification:

> **Rom 4:6-8**
> **emphasis added**
>
> David says the same thing when he speaks of the blessedness of the one to whom **God credits righteousness** apart from works: 'Blessed are those whose transgressions are forgiven, whose sins are covered. Blessed is the one whose sin **the Lord will never count against them**'.

Here are the two aspects of justification: (1) God does not count, or impute, people's sin against them, and (2) he counts, or imputes, righteousness to people.

The first aspect of justification is the remission, or forgiveness, of sins. God, through Christ's substitutionary death on the cross (Rom 3:25; 5:9), does not reckon people's sins against them, which is a legal notion through and through. Christ has atoned for all their sins – past, present, and future – and God declares them "not guilty." With reference to those who embrace the gospel, "therefore there is now no condemnation for those who are in Christ Jesus" (Rom 8:1).

The second aspect of justification is the imputation of righteousness: God reckons people righteous, not because they actually are righteous in themselves or through their good works meriting righteousness for them, but because he credits the righteousness of his Son to them. Paul underscores this point with his contrast between Adam and Christ: "For just as through the disobedience of the one man the many were made sinners, so also through the obedience of the one man the many will be made righteous" (Rom 5:19). By association with Adam and his disobedience, all people are "made sinners" – a legal term referring to their dismal, guilty status before God. Oppositely, by association with Christ and his obedience, all who repent of their sins and trust Christ by faith are "made righteous" – again a legal term referring to their new, justified status before God. Christ undid the disobedience of Adam by obeying the Father perfectly, and the Father imputes his Son's perfect righteousness to all who embrace the gospel.

A beautiful example of such imputation of righteousness as justification is Abraham:

Gen 15:1-6

> *After this, the word of the Lord came to Abram in a vision: 'Do not be afraid, Abram. I am your shield, your very great reward. But Abram said, 'Sovereign Lord, what can you give me since I remain childless and the one who will inherit my estate is Eliezer of Damascus?' And Abram said, 'You have given me no children; so a servant in my household will be my heir.' Then the word of the Lord came to him: 'This man will not be your heir, but a son who is your own flesh and blood will be your heir.' He took him outside and said, 'Look up at the sky and count the stars – if indeed you can count them.' Then he said to him, 'So shall your offspring be.' Abram believed the Lord, and he credited it to him as righteousness.*

Abraham was not in a good spot. Though God had promised that he would become the father of a great nation (Gen 12:1-3), the "patriarch" was childless, with only Eliezer as his heir. Hearing Abraham's complaint, God specified Abraham's own son would instead be his heir, in fulfilment of the divine promise. As Abraham stood on the verge of taking matters into his own hands and establishing Eliezer as his heir, he instead trusted God to fulfil his promise. And God credited Abraham's faith as righteousness. The ungodly, unrighteous patriarch, as he believed the divine promise, was declared righteous before God. The significance of this for us is drawn out by Paul at the end of Romans chapter 4, where Abraham emerges as our example. His justification is the model for our justification:

Rom 4:22-25

> *This is why 'it was credited to him as righteousness.' The words 'it was credited to him' were written not for him alone, but also for us, to whom God will credit righteousness – for us who believe in him who raised Jesus our Lord from the dead. He was delivered over to death for our sins and was raised to life for our justification.*

Key differences between the Catholic and Protestant positions

1. The nature of justification

Building on Paul's discussion in Rom 4, Protestant theology maintains justification is the legal declaration that ungodly people are "not guilty" but "righteous" instead. Their standing before God is established because God no longer counts their sins against them because of the work of his Son, and because God counts his Son's righteousness to them. Accordingly, justification is not, as Catholic theology holds, "not only the remission of sins, but also the sanctification and renewal of the interior man." This Catholic view, which fuses forgiveness, sanctification, and regeneration, does not reflect the biblical affirmations about justification as a divine, legal declaration.

2. The role of grace

Second, Catholic theology emphasises the initiating role of grace, insisting that "no one can merit the initial grace of forgiveness and justification." This position seems to concur with what has just been written about the divine initiative in salvation. However, Protestant theology disagrees with the Catholic notion of a preparatory, or prevenient, grace which goes before all people and prompts them to receive more grace for conversion leading to justification. The reason for dismissing this species of grace is the fact that Scripture itself does not affirm it.

CCC 2010.

3. The meaning and the means of grace

More importantly, however, is that the Catholic perspective on grace and the Protestant view of grace are at odds. Yes, both agree that grace is unmerited favour and help. But Catholic theology views grace and nature as being interdependent, meaning grace must be communicated through concrete natural elements. In the Catholic Church, these elements are its sacraments using consecrated water, oil, bread, and wine. Specifically, as we have observed, "Justification is conferred in Baptism, the sacrament of faith." In the sacrament of Baptism, as the priest pours consecrated water on the infant's head, grace is infused and that baby is cleansed of original sin, regenerated, and incorporated into Christ and his Church. In the sacrament of Confirmation, when that infant turns ten years old (this is just an example, as the age may differ), the priest administers consecrated oil by which grace is infused and that young person is bound more closely to the Church and receives a fresh outpouring of the Spirit. In the sacrament of the Eucharist, as that ten year old participates in her first communion, the priest gives her the consecrated bread and wine by which grace is infused and that young person's union with Christ is augmented and she is separated from sin. The grace of God is communicated through the consecrated elements of nature, the sacraments, and the ten year old – that is, all the Catholic faithful – receive an infusion of grace by which their nature is transformed, enabling them to merit eternal life. The view of grace differs significantly between Catholic and Protestant theology.

Whereas Catholic theology emphasises that justification is conferred in the sacrament of Baptism (the sacrament of faith), Protestant theology insists justification is appropriated by faith alone. Indeed, this is the material principle of Protestantism: justification by grace alone through faith alone. Certainly, Protestant churches and denominations differ as to their understanding and practice of baptism, but the majority of them do not link justification with baptism, certainly not in the way that Catholic theology does.

Once again, the case of Abraham is decisive on this point:

CCC 1992.

The formal & material principles

Theologians sometimes distinguish between the *formal* principle and the *material* principle. The formal principle describes the authoritative source of your theology – *how* you know what you know. For the Reformation, this is *sola scriptura*. The material principle describes the central doctrine – *what* you know and place centrally. For the Reformation, this is justification *sola fide* and *sola gratia*.

For more on the *sola* terms, see Matthew Barrett's article (p6).

Rom 4:1-5

> What then shall we say that Abraham, our forefather according to the flesh, discovered in this matter? If, in fact, Abraham was justified by works, he had something to boast about – but not before God. What does Scripture say? 'Abraham believed God, and it was credited to him as righteousness.' Now to the one who works, wages are not credited as a gift but as an obligation. However, to the one who does not work but trusts God who justifies the ungodly, their faith is credited as righteousness.

When a person works, he earns wages, the payment contracted and thus due for work performed. Paul underscores how ludicrous is the idea that Abraham was justified by the good works he did, for he would be in the position to boast about his accomplishment as a godly man. But who can boast before God? No one, and certainly not Abraham! He was an idol worshipper from Ur who did not work but believed in God who does not justify the godly, but the ungodly (Rom 4:5). Abraham was justified by faith and not by works. Paul confirms this point, underscoring Abraham's justification came before he was circumcised (Rom 4:10-11) and apart from the law, which came much later (Rom 4:13). Thus, the idea of being justified before God by works – participation in the sacraments, engagement in good deeds – is wrongheaded. Justification is by faith, and faith alone.

4. Co-operation

Catholic theology is synergistic: both God and the faithful work together to accomplish salvation. God acts powerfully and provides grace for justification. The faithful give "the assent of faith to the Word of God," respond with conversion, and obey "the prompting of the Holy Spirit who precedes and preserves [their] assent." By contrast, evangelical theology's doctrine of justification is monergistic. God, and God alone, justifies the ungodly (Rom 4:5), who cannot contribute anything to their justification. God, and God alone, declares the unrighteous "not guilty" but "righteous" instead. Monergism, not synergism, is the proper framework for justification by grace through faith.

CCC 1993.

5. A place for merit?

Indeed, this monergistic framework critiques the Catholic notion of merit (the recompense that God owes to the faithful as they cooperate with divine grace to engage in good works). Though Catholic theology insists "no one can merit the initial grace of forgiveness and justification," the Catholic faithful, prompted by the Holy Spirit and love, achieve for themselves and for others the grace for continued sanctification, the increase of grace and love, and the attainment of eternal life.

CCC 2010.

Protestant theology denies any possibility of attaining grace and considers human effort toward the meriting of eternal life to be superfluous. The doctrine of justification leaves no room, nor need, for merit: as God declares the ungodly "not guilty" but "righteous" instead, their eternal life is based not on this gracious act of God plus their own effort (even effort prompted and steadied by divine grace), but on God's declaration alone received by faith alone. They are reckoned completely righteous because God has imputed the perfect righteousness of Christ to them by faith. What could they possibly add to this salvation? Nothing at all. How could they possibly merit eternal life? They cannot. Out of thankfulness for their standing before God through justification, and as the fruit of their new nature through regeneration and sanctification, they engage in good works, which

God, and God alone, justifies the ungodly

God himself will richly reward – grace upon grace! Such rewards, however, have nothing to do with merit as Catholic theology understands that idea.

6. The perseverance of the saints and assurance of salvation

Noted briefly above, Catholic theology holds that the Catholic faithful, though undergirded by divine grace, can resist that grace and lose their salvation. Indeed, mortal sin results in the loss of grace and demands a fresh infusion of it through the sacrament of Penance. Protestant theology, by contrast, insists that genuine Christians, though they may temporarily fall into sin, will emerge from their worldliness and return to walking with God and bearing fruit. This is the doctrine of the perseverance of the saints: all genuine Christians (not those who merely profess to be saved) are protected by the power of God operating through their faith for ultimate salvation (1 Pet. 1:5). Perseverance is the divine work by which God preserves those whom he has elected and saved. On the basis of that empowering activity, Christians enjoy the privilege of the assurance of salvation, which is their subjective confidence that they are now, and will continue to be forever, children of God (Rom 8:16). Catholic theology, with its misunderstanding of justification, denies such assurance of salvation to be possible.

CCC 1993.

CCC 1446.

Westminster Confession of Faith, ch. 17.

Conclusion

Justification, the material principle of the Reformation, continues to be a doctrine of wide divergence between Roman Catholicism and Protestantism.

- *The definition of justification differs between the two traditions.*

- *The nature of grace that is at the heart of justification separates Catholic theology and Protestant theology.*

- *The appropriation of justification – by faith plus baptism, or by faith alone – is a major disagreement.*

- *Whether salvation is synergistic, featuring both a divine role and a human role, or monergistic, wrought by God alone, distinguishes the two traditions.*

- *Merit, while prominent in the Catholic view of justification, is absent from the Protestant view.*

- *And Catholic theology denies the perseverance of the saints, along with its corollary, the assurance of salvation, while Protestant theology embraces them.*

Gregg Allison and Chris Castaldo, *The Unfinished Reformation: What Unites and Divides Catholics and Protestants after 500 Years* (Grand Rapids: Zondervan, 2016).

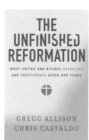

In this Reformation anniversary year, we have to say that each of these points matter. For that reason, Chris Castaldo and I recently published a book entitled *The Unfinished Reformation*. We rejoice that the battles between Catholics and Protestants taking place at the time of the Reformation have given way to more civilised dispute and, at times, even honest dialogue between the two traditions. But the Reformation is unfinished for many reasons, not the least of which is the persistent divergence over the doctrine of justification. The implication for us evangelicals is to continue what we have always done: share the evangel – the gospel – with all people: those from both Catholic and Protestant backgrounds, as well as Muslims, Buddhists, Hindus, agnostics, atheists, and more. Specifically, as we engage Catholics with the good news, we should be attentive to the many commonalities that unite us: belief in the triune God, the deity and humanity of Jesus Christ, the person and work of the Holy Spirit, and much more. Indeed, we may find some Catholics who, through hearing Scripture read at mass, or by being involved in a Bible study, or because of friendships with evangelicals, have truly grasped the gospel. But we must also be forthcoming about our differences. We must call upon Catholics to cease relying on everything they are seeking to do to cooperate with divine grace in order to merit eternal life, and to rely on Christ alone through grace alone by faith alone. Only in this way will God justify them, even as he has justified us.

This wide gulf of division between the Catholic and Protestant understandings of justification was vividly portrayed in the Roman Catholic Church's Year of Mercy. Ultimately it comes down to this: Can the Catholic faithful obtain plenary indulgences through their cooperative efforts with the grace of God, resulting in release from purgatory for themselves and others who are not perfectly righteous? Or does God graciously declare ungodly people "not guilty" but "righteous" instead, resulting in release from condemnation and the gift of perfect righteousness?

Protestants, too, have a door of mercy: Jesus Christ, the righteous one. Through Christ alone, grace alone, and faith alone, all who embrace the gospel are justified forever before God. P

standing still?

The doctrine of justification and the debates of the last half century
by David Starling

Apparently Luther never said

"Here I stand"

at the climax of his speech before the Diet of Worms. But stand he did, nonetheless, and at great cost and personal risk.

Those words were, it seems, added into Luther's closing speech by the editor of the published edition that Luther had printed later that year.

The council convened by the Holy Roman Emperor in 1521, to pass judgment on allegations of heresy made against Luther. *Worms* (pronounced 'Vorms') is a place in Germany. In this context, *diet* means an assembly. So the *Diet of Worms* is the meeting where Luther took his stand. A diet of worms is what birds eat.

Among the many heresies alleged against Luther, there was nothing that amounted to an explicit statement of the doctrine of justification by faith alone. But many of them were the outworkings of the new understanding of God's saving righteousness that he had arrived at as he prepared his lectures on Romans and Psalms in the middle years of the preceding decade. And increasingly, across the decades that followed, his assertions regarding the nature and basis of justification came to be understood as the defining issue over which Luther and his fellow reformers took their stand and suffered excommunication from the church of Rome. This doctrine, Luther insisted, was a hill worth dying on...

> **"** ...because if this article [of justification] stands, the church stands; if this article falls, the church falls.

WA 40/3.352.3. Cited in Alister E. McGrath, *Iustitia Dei: A History of the Christian Doctrine of Justification*, 2nd ed. (Cambridge: Cambridge University Press, 1998), 450.

By the beginning of the seventeenth century, among both Lutheran and Reformed theologians, Luther's assertion had begun to function as a kind of proverb and theological first principle. According to Johann Heinrich Alsted, for example (writing in 1618), the doctrine of justification was "said to be the article by which the church stands or falls."

Johann Heinrich Alsted, *Theologia scholastica didacta* [Hanover, 1618], 711, cited in *Iustitia Dei*, 450.

If the claim is expressed in its later, proverbial, form, then there are questions that ought to be asked about the way in which it isolates and elevates the doctrine of justification as the *only* doctrine by which the health of the church is determined. But if the claim is made in its earlier form, as Luther framed it, then it is not difficult to find New Testament precedent. Justification by faith, in and of itself, is not the gospel, but it is an inseparable entailment of the gospel announcements about the saving death and resurrection of Jesus. A version of the gospel that proclaims Christ's death and resurrection but goes on to insist that men and women are justified by some other means than faith in him is, in Paul's words, "a gospel other than the one we preached to you" (Gal 1:8); it is a gospel that comes with the implication that "Christ died for nothing" (Gal 2:21).

So Luther was right in his insistence that the doctrine of justification is a doctrine worth taking a stand for. But the kind of stand Luther took before the Diet of Worms was not like Colonel Custer's – a death-or-glory, ask-no-questions defence of territory, blazing away at all comers. By turning up at the Diet, Luther was submitting to the scrutiny of his assertions, just as he had originally invited it when he nailed his theses to the door of the Wittenberg church. Even his closing words expressed a willingness to be convinced "by Scripture and plain reason" of any error in what he had written. Thus, to stand with Luther is not to turn his assertions into unquestionable dogma, but to join with him in the task of responding to the various questions that might be asked about what the Protestant doctrine of justification means and whether it is true.

And the last five centuries have not been short on questions. In this article, I will restrict my focus to just the last fifty years (or, more precisely, to the last fifty-four years, since the publication in 1963 of Krister Stendahl's landmark article on "The Apostle Paul and the Introspective Conscience of the West"). After sketching a brief summary of some of the main questions that New Testament scholars have asked about justification during this period, I will offer a brief response in which I will attempt to show how we might go about answering them, what we can learn from them, and what conclusions we might draw regarding the shape of Christian faith and life.

Krister Stendahl, "The Apostle Paul and the Introspective Conscience of the West," *HTR* 56, no. 3 (1963).

five questions which have posed challenges to a traditional reading of justification

1. Have we misread Paul by assuming Luther was asking the right questions?

As Matthew Barrett's article shows, Luther's monastic life generated anxious questions about whether he could be saved – he had an "introspective conscience" desperate for assurance. Stendahl's article argued that this was not the case for Paul. He had a 'robust' conscience, both before and after his conversion, and so we shouldn't read those more medieval anxieties back into Paul.

The lasting influence of Stendahl's article, however, had more to do with hermeneutics than psychology. His challenge was, most basically, to the deeply-ingrained, centuries-old Protestant habit of interpreting Paul's context by analogy with Luther's:

> " *The Reformers' interpretation of Paul rests on an analogism when Pauline statements about Faith and Works, Law and Gospel, Jews and Gentiles are read in the framework of late medieval piety. The Law, the Torah, with its specific requirements of circumcision and food restrictions becomes a general principle of 'legalism' in religious matters. Where Paul was concerned about the possibility for Gentiles to be included in the messianic community, his statements are now read as answers to the quest for assurance about man's salvation out of a common human predicament.*

"Apostle Paul," 205-6.

The origins of Stendahl's famous article were in an address to the American Psychological Association, and its immediate focus was on the psychological question of whether Paul can legitimately be claimed as "the hero of the introspective conscience." ("Apostle Paul," 199.) His address included a sharp critique of modern attempts to read Paul's letters (and particularly his depiction of the anguished "I" in Rom 7:14-25) as psychological autobiography and understand Paul's gospel as an attempt to resolve universal human experiences of guilt and self-recrimination.

i.e. interpretation of the Bible

Luther's question, Stendahl argued, was the question of the anxious, late medieval conscience: "How can I find a gracious God?" Paul's questions, on the other hand, were questions that arose out of the twists and turns of salvation history and the missionary experience of proclaiming the Jewish Messiah among the Gentiles:

Stendahl, "Apostle Paul," 204.

1) What happens to the Law (the Torah, the actual Law of Moses, not the principle of legalism) when the Messiah has come?

2) What are the ramifications of the Messiah's arrival for the relation between Jews and Gentiles?

You can hear the influence of Stendahl whenever someone says that we need to read the New Testament afresh, asking 1st century questions, rather than coming to it with 16th century questions and assumptions.

Reading Paul's letters as if he were answering Luther's question was, according to Stendahl, a fundamental interpretive error. For Stendahl, we need to see that Paul's doctrine of justification is addressed to Paul's questions: how Jews and Gentiles relate, rather than how men and women stand before God.

2. What does it mean that justification is "not... by the works of the law"?

Paul among Jews and Gentiles, and Other Essays (Philadelphia: Fortress, 1976).

Stendahl's article had an immediate influence when it was published in 1963, and it received a second life a decade later when it was republished as one of the chapters in his book, *Paul among Jews and Gentiles*. The publication of that book in 1976 was just in time for it to contribute to the late-1970s crescendo of scholarly debate regarding understandings of law and grace in Second Temple Judaism and their implications for our interpretation of Paul.

That is, Judaism from the time in which the Jerusalem temple was rebuilt around 516BC to its destruction in AD70.

E. P. Sanders, *Paul and Palestinian Judaism: A Comparison between Patterns of Religion* (Philadelphia: Fortress, 1977).

Another influential contribution to that debate came the following year, with E. P. Sanders' book, *Paul and Palestinian Judaism*. Sanders built on the earlier work of scholars, and attempted to demolish once and for all the traditional portrayal of Judaism in Protestant New Testament studies as a religion of legalistic merit-making which treated it as a direct parallel to medieval Catholicism. Against the long-held assumption that Second Temple Judaism could be seen as a paradigm for grace-less legalism, Sanders argued that the pattern of religion believed and practised by Second Temple Jews could better be described as a kind of *covenantal nomism*. He coined this term to describe a pattern of religion in which the individual's obedience to the law ('nomism') was embedded within the larger framework of a covenant God had established by grace:

> **"** The "pattern" or 'structure' of covenantal nomism is this: (1) God has chosen Israel and (2) given the law. The law implies both (3) God's promise to maintain the election and (4) the requirement to obey. (5) God rewards obedience and punishes transgression. (6) The law provides for means of atonement, and atonement results in (7) maintenance or re-establishment of the covenantal relationship. (8) All those who are maintained in the covenant by obedience, atonement and God's mercy belong to the group which will be saved. An important interpretation of the first and last points is that election and ultimately salvation are considered to be by God's mercy rather than human achievement.

Sanders, *Paul and Palestinian Judaism*, 422.

This understanding of Second Temple Judaism had obvious implications for the interpretation of Paul's letters: "On the point at which many have found the decisive contrast between Paul and Judaism – grace and works – Paul is in agreement with Palestinian Judaism." As James Dunn put it, a decade and a half later:

Paul and Palestinian Judaism, 543, 154-55.

> **"** The Judaism of what Sanders christened as "covenantal nomism" can now be seen to preach good Protestant doctrine: that grace is always prior; that human effort is ever the response to divine initiative; that good works are the fruit and not the root of salvation.

James D. G. Dunn and Alan M. Suggate, *The Justice of God: A Fresh Look at the Old Doctrine of Justification by Faith* (Carlisle: Paternoster, 1993), 8.

This new perspective on Judaism raises a key question: if Judaism preached salvation by grace, then what was Paul opposed to when he denied justification by works? Although Sanders' own attempts to answer that question were widely criticised, his work provided the catalyst for a series of important studies of Pauline theology in the late 1970s and early 1980s. The most influential of these were by N. T. Wright and James Dunn, who christened the emerging paradigm as "the New Perspective on Paul."

The New Perspective on Paul is a varied and complicated beast. We've tried to lay out the main ideas here but if you want to dig a bit deeper, Stephen Westerholm is a helpful guide – try his short overview: *Justification Reconsidered: Rethinking a Pauline Theme* (Grand Rapids: Eerdmans, 2013).

One major theme in the early writings of Dunn and Wright was the meaning of *works of the law* in Second Temple Judaism and in Paul's letters. According to both Dunn and Wright (as they expressed the view in those early writings) the works of the law are not good works in general, but rather "*covenant* works... particular observances of the law like circumcision and food laws." The function of such works of the law, Dunn argued, was not the amassing of merit, but rather the maintenance of the boundaries of the covenant people:

James D. G. Dunn, "The New Perspective on Paul," *BJRL* 65 (1983): 107, emphasis original.

Works of the law are nowhere understood here, either by his Jewish interlocutors or by Paul himself, as works which earn God's favour, as merit-amassing observances. They are rather seen as badges; they are simply what membership of the covenant people involves, what mark out the Jews as God's people. ..."Works of the law" do not mean "good works" in general... in the sense of self-achievement. The phrase "works of the law" in Gal 2:16 is, in fact, a fairly restricted one; it refers precisely to those same identity markers described above... circumcision, food laws and sabbath.

"New Perspective," 109-11. In their later writings, Dunn and Wright have both granted the argument of their critics that "works of the law" in Paul's writing (and in Second Temple Jewish usage more generally) is unlikely to have been understood as referring narrowly and exclusively to identity-marking works such as these. The reading of Paul's "works of the law" language that Dunn and Wright tend to argue for in their later writings is that it refers more broadly to conduct in conformity with the stipulations of the law of Moses, but that (especially when used in contexts of controversy over communal boundaries) it was used in ways that emphasised the identity-marking function of Torah-obedience. See especially "New Perspective View," in Justification: Five Views, ed. James K. Beilby and Paul R. Eddy (Downers Grove: IVP, 2011), esp. 194, and N. T. Wright, Paul and the Faithfulness of God (London: SPCK, 2013), 1027-35.

Paul's criticism of Judaism therefore, has nothing to do with legalism. To speak against works of the law is not to criticise attempts to earn God's favour. Rather, it is to criticise Jewish exclusivity – they proudly wore those badges and saw themselves as different from the Gentiles because of them. Their sin was *ethnocentrism*. And for the New Perspective, that is wrong now that Christ has come. Paul's message is that faith is the new badge and anyone, Jew or Gentile, can wear that.

3. How does justification relate to covenant?

Whilst Dunn and Wright both criticised Sanders for his failure to rethink the meaning of works of the law in Paul's letters, Wright went on to criticise him for failing to rethink justification itself: "One of the many odd things about Sanders' presentation of Paul is that he never really considers whether Paul might mean something other by justification than that which the tradition has suggested."

"Justification by Faith: Can We Get It Right Now?," *Tyndale Biblical Theology Lecture* (1994): 1.

Again, it comes back to Sanders' work. If the Jews did believe that they were God's people because of God's gracious act making them his people, then whatever *justification by faith and not by works of the law* means, it cannot be answering the question of how people are saved.

For Wright, the key was the context of the dispute in Galatia that produced Paul's earliest pronouncements on justification. In Galatians, Paul deploys justification to settle questions of the dining room, not the courtroom (see especially Gal 2:11-15). For Wright, this shows that the main issue is whether Jew and Gentile are on equal terms. Consequently, Paul's argument is that now that Christ has come, everyone is marked out as belonging to God's people by wearing the faith badge and so should unite and eat together. Read in that context, Wright sees justification very differently: to be justified by faith means that faith (rather than those other badges) marks a person out as belonging to God's people. Faith signals one's *covenant membership*, and to be justified means to be *found to be in the covenant*. Justification by faith should therefore (according to Wright, particularly in his early writings) be understood not primarily as a soteriological doctrine ("How do I find a gracious God?") but as an ecclesiological doctrine ("Who are the true people of God, and what are the boundary-markers that define who belongs?"):

N. T. Wright, "Justification: Yesterday, Today, and Forever," *JETS* 54 (2011): 56.

i.e. addressing issues of salvation.

i.e. addressing issues of the church.

This is the thrust of the Pauline doctrine of justification: it is not a scheme of thought about how persons find a relationship with God, but the truth that all who believe in Jesus belong at the same table, no matter what their racial or moral background. Ironically, in terms of Protestant polemic, Paul's doctrine is more about ecclesiology than about soteriology.

"Justification by Faith," 13. The irony, for Wright, lies in the fact that justification (as he understands its meaning in Paul's letters) is the ecumenical doctrine that should bring together everyone confessing Jesus as Lord, yet it is precisely this doctrine that has become the principal fault-line separating Protestants from Catholics.

4. Is justification a verdict or a process?

Wright's interpretation of Paul (in common with the various proposals of the New Perspective on Paul more generally) has a tendency to criticise the way in which Protestant polemics have traditionally functioned as the lens through which Paul should be read. His own reading of Paul's view of justification, however, is hardly an attempt to reinstate the pre-Reformation or Tridentine Catholic view that justification involves an inward renewal, rather than a verdict God makes about someone.

That is, the view represented by the Council of Trent. For more on that, see Gregg Allison's article (p35).

Others, however, have attempted to combine a covenantal reading of justification, reminiscent of Wright's, with a re-opening of the old question about whether justification in Paul refers to a verdict of acquittal, a process of moral transformation, or some combination of the two. One notable contemporary example is Michael Gorman, who attempts to meld together elements of Catholic, Protestant and New Perspective understandings into a single, composite definition. According to Gorman, the meaning of justification in Paul's letters is "the establishment or restoration of right covenant relations – fidelity to God and love for neighbour – with the certain hope of acquittal/vindication on the day of judgment."

Michael J. Gorman, *Inhabiting the Cruciform God: Kenosis, Justification, and Theosis in Paul's Narrative Soteriology* (Grand Rapids: Eerdmans, 2009), 53.

Gorman's enquiry into Paul's understanding of justification is framed, in part, by ecumenical and exegetical issues. He suspects that Protestant interpretations have gone astray by attempting to press Paul's letters into polemical service against Catholicism, and he is concerned that this has entrenched divisions that could otherwise have been bridged.

i.e. issues relating to unity among different Christian churches and issues arising from the text of Scripture.

Alongside these issues, though, is the question of how our understanding of justification shapes the way we view (and live) the Christian life. Put at its sharpest, the question Gorman poses is whether an understanding of justification that focuses entirely on law-court imagery might be not just a divisive doctrine, or an exegetically unfounded one, but a "dangerous" doctrine, fostering the disease of "cheap justification", i.e. "justification without justice, faith without love, declaration without transformation."

Reading Paul, 115-6; *Inhabiting the Cruciform God*, 41.

5. What kind of God lies behind theories of justification?

If Gorman's account of justification is an attempt to create a kind of hybrid out of Catholic, Protestant and New Perspective approaches to the doctrine, the final view in our brief survey of fifty years' worth of scholarly debate attempts to sweep them all aside and replace them with something altogether different. It has become known as the *apocalyptic* version of justification, and is most thoroughly defended by Douglas Campbell.

According to Campbell, the common failing of all versions of "justification theory" – Catholic and Protestant alike – is their assumption that in the background of God's saving righteousness lies a retributive God, rendering punishment to wrongdoers according to the measure of their guilt. To read Paul in this way, Campbell argues, is to make the mistake of hearing a conventional recital of the logic of retribution in Romans 1:18-3:20 as if it were Paul's own view when in fact (according to Campbell) it should be read as Paul's mocking parody of the failed, dead-end logic of Paul's opponents.

According to Campbell, the focus of God's justice is not on the just punishment of wrongdoers but the overthrow of oppressive powers. Justification is therefore a verdict, but the sphere within which it operates is not the "forensic-retributive" sphere within which God who offers pardon to the guilty on the condition that they join themselves by faith to Christ, whose perfect righteousness and unmerited death satisfy the demands of divine retribution. Rather, justification operates within "forensic-liberative" sphere, executing a verdict against enslaving powers and announcing a universal, unconditional divine deliverance of humanity accomplished in the resurrection of Jesus from the dead.

For more detail on his argument and a review, see Douglas J. Moo, "Review Article: The Deliverance of God: An Apocalyptic Rereading of Justification in Paul by Douglas A. Campbell," *JETS* 53 (2010): 143–50 (available as a PDF online).

What follows is based on the summary of "Justification Theory," as Campbell understands it, in Douglas A. Campbell, *The Deliverance of God: An Apocalyptic Rereading of Justification in Paul* (Grand Rapids: Eerdmans, 2009), 11-35.

responding and learning

In different ways, the questions outlined above have posed a challenge to the traditional Protestant understanding of justification. In what follows I will offer a few very brief thoughts on what can be learned from each of the questions noted above, and how we might answer the challenges that they pose.

1. Have we misread Paul by assuming Luther was asking the right questions?

There is wisdom in Stendahl's warning against the danger of reading Paul as if he were attempting in the first century to answer the questions of the sixteenth. It would be a mistake, though, to read Paul's letters as if the *only* issue worth reflecting on for him was the place of Gentiles within the community of the Messiah, or as if he (and the writers of the Old Testament Scriptures before him) were uninterested in the predicament of the individual sinner – or, for that matter, the community as a whole – in the face of the judgment of God. The picture that Paul paints in Romans 1:18-3:20, for example, is not only a picture of *Jew and Gentile together* under the judgment of God; it is, equally, a picture of Jew and Gentile together *under the judgment of God*. The gospel that he preached to the Thessalonians was not simply a summons to turn from idols and serve the living and true God; it was also, equally, an announcement about Jesus, the risen Son, as the one who "rescues us from the coming wrath" (1 Thess 1:10).

2. What does it mean that justification is "not... by the works of the law"?

Sanders' challenge to the deep-rooted Protestant habit of reconstructing a legalistic first-century Judaism as a foil for Paul's gospel of grace is, likewise, a helpful corrective to a centuries-long pattern of reductionism and distortion. But as a number of scholars have noted, there is also a tendency towards over-simplification in Sanders' own account. Second Temple Judaism was more variegated than Sanders' covenantal nomism suggests, and in at least some strands of Second Temple Judaism there was a belief that the restoration of the nation or the individual's continuing experience of divine favour (and post-mortem fate) was conditional on their meritorious obedience to the law. The Pharisee whom Jesus depicts at prayer in the temple in Luke 18:9-14 is "confident of [his] own righteousness", and bases that confidence on how different he is from "robbers, evildoers, adulterers", and how faithful he is in his fasting and tithing. Unless Jesus (and Luke after him) was fundamentally out of touch with the Judaism of his day, one can only assume that there must have been real-life Pharisees whose prayers resembled those of the Pharisee in the parable, and a real possibility that some amongst the audience who heard the parable would have been shocked by the parable's punchline – that it was the tax collector, and not the Pharisee, who "went home justified before God" (v. 14).

3. How does justification relate to covenant?

Dunn and Wright's work has been valuable in highlighting the boundary-marking functions that Torah-observance served within Second Temple Judaism and the relevance of such questions for disputes about circumcision and table fellowship within the first-century church. They are right to insist, too, that Paul's view of justification has implications for our own contemporary boundary-marking disputes and tribal divisions. But (as they themselves grant) the same premises that Paul builds on to settle an argument about circumcision and table fellowship can also form the basis for a larger theological argument against any form of religion that makes human works the basis for divine justification. And (probably to a greater extent than Dunn and Wright would grant) the basic outlines of that larger, more generalised argument against *any* kind of human works as a basis for justification and *any* kind of boasting as a legitimate human posture in the presence of God can already be found within the logic of Paul's own letters. Paul can (and does, in his letters to the Galatians and the Romans) address a dispute about table fellowship with an argument about soteriology, reminding his readers of the basis on which human beings, whoever they are, can find themselves welcomed by God and not condemned under his judgment (Rom 14:3-4), experiencing his blessing and not his curse (Gal 3:1-14).

Paul's criticism of works of the law as a basis for justification relates to *both* their function as membership badges (e.g. Rom 2:17-24) *and* their status as moral achievements (e.g. Rom 4:4-6); the reason why God has not appointed them as the path to justification has to do with *both* their exclusivity (e.g. Rom 3:29) *and* the inability of Israel – or anyone – to perform them adequately (e.g. Rom 3:20; 4:14); the consequences of justification by faith include *both* covenant membership (e.g. Gal 3:24-29) *and* peace with God (e.g. Rom 5:1).

4. Is justification a verdict or a process?

Openness to both/and statements of this sort is, in general, a good thing, given the complexity of life and the tendency of academic argument to generate false dichotomies. But not all both/and proposals have merit. In the case of justification, there is still good reason to keep insisting on the essentially forensic metaphor implied by the way in which the word is used within the New Testament (and more broadly, in the great majority of Graeco-Roman and Second Temple Jewish usage). The opposite of *justify*, in biblical usage, is *condemn* (e.g. Deut 25:1; Rom 8:33-34), and the context that is consistently implied (and frequently explicit) when the verb is used is a courtroom, either literal or figurative, in which the positive or negative verdict is pronounced. Gorman's warning against the dangers of a 'cheap' account of God's saving purposes is gravely important, but the broad, inclusive definition of justification that he offers as a remedy simply does not fit the evidence of the New Testament. Other remedies exist, as I will argue below, but this remedy is not the right one.

In the Graeco-Roman literature, the Greek verb *dikaioō* (when used with a personal object) generally refers to the action of punishing or otherwise doing justice to a wrongdoer, rather than to the acquittal or vindication of the innocent (which is its commonest meaning in the Jewish literature). But in both bodies of literature the word is still used, in the great majority of instances, to refer to an act of judgment within a literal or metaphorical courtroom.

5. What kind of God lies behind theories of justification?

The questions raised by Campbell's apocalyptic account of justification are also worth paying attention to. It is true, as he emphasises, that Paul frequently speaks about sin as an oppressive, enslaving power, and of God's salvation as an act of gracious, sovereign deliverance from that enslavement. Occasionally (e.g. Rom 6:7) Paul can use the language of justification to speak of a liberating verdict of that sort. But the attempt that Campbell makes to sever the verdict of justification from all connections with the demands of God's retributive justice requires a reading of Rom 1:18-3:20 that is so elaborate and counter-intuitive that (as far as we know) not a single interpreter between Paul's time and Campbell's has been capable of discovering it. A reading that ingenious may be clever, but it is unlikely to be convincing.

final remarks

Two remarks of a more general nature are worth making as I close.

The first is about the place of justification within the larger landscape of Paul's soteriology and his vision of God's righteousness. One reason, I suspect, why so many attempts are made to reimagine the meaning of Paul's justification language is the centuries-old tendency of theologians to fixate on justification as if it were the totality of what Paul had to say about the saving work of God in the world and the revelation of his righteousness. Justification, as Garwood Anderson puts it, "is like a man with three full-time jobs surrounded on every side by the underemployed."

Anderson, *Paul's New Perspective*, 384-85.

Even if we put to one side for a moment Paul's salvation and sanctification language, and focus just on righteousness, there is still much more to be said than can be contained within the forensic language that speaks about the justification of believers.

The verb *to justify* is consistently forensic in Paul, referring to a verdict that declares believers to be free from divine condemnation and free from the oppressive dominion of sin and death (e.g. Rom 6:7). But righteousness language, as Paul employs it in Romans, can refer to realities that take place before, during and after the metaphorical law court in which the verdict of justification is pronounced. For Paul, the active, ethical righteousness of the life that is transformed by obedient faith and participates in the manifestation of God's righteousness on earth is not only the evidence of salvation but an integral dimension of its content and purpose (cf. Rom 8:4). Believers are saved in order that they might live a new life, in which they offer every part of themselves to God as "an instrument [or, better, 'weapon'] of righteousness" (Rom 6:13).

This emphasis continues through the rest of the letter, especially in chapters 12-16, where Paul impresses upon his readers the outworking that his gospel ought to have within their social relationships: "The kingdom of God," Paul reminds his readers, "is not a matter of eating and drinking, but of righteousness, peace and joy in the Holy Spirit" (Rom 14:17).

If we restrict our account of the gospel's implications to the doctrine of justification alone, then our view of salvation will inevitably be a thin and dangerously truncated one; if we attempt to remedy that problem by redefining justification to include all of the apocalyptic and transformative themes that we find lacking in one-dimensionally forensic accounts of the gospel, then we end up with a bloated notion of justification that can no longer perform the particular task that belongs to it.

This leads to a second, concluding, remark, about the special work that the doctrine of justification by grace alone, through faith alone, does perform within Paul's letters. Justification is not the sum total of the gospel's entailments as Paul traces them out within his letters. But it is, nonetheless, a precious and critically important one. Where it is proclaimed and believed (in all of its proper connections with the saving rule of the crucified and risen Jesus, the gospel's summons to repentance and faith, and the promise of the transforming work of the Spirit) Paul's doctrine of justification plays a powerful role in destroying all false and divisive human boasting, replacing it with a joyful, humble assurance and a gracious, hospitable welcome to fellow-believers who have been justified by the same grace.

It is an indispensable doctrine for the life and health of the church, worth standing *for*, in courageous faithfulness, and standing *on*, in confidence and joy. P

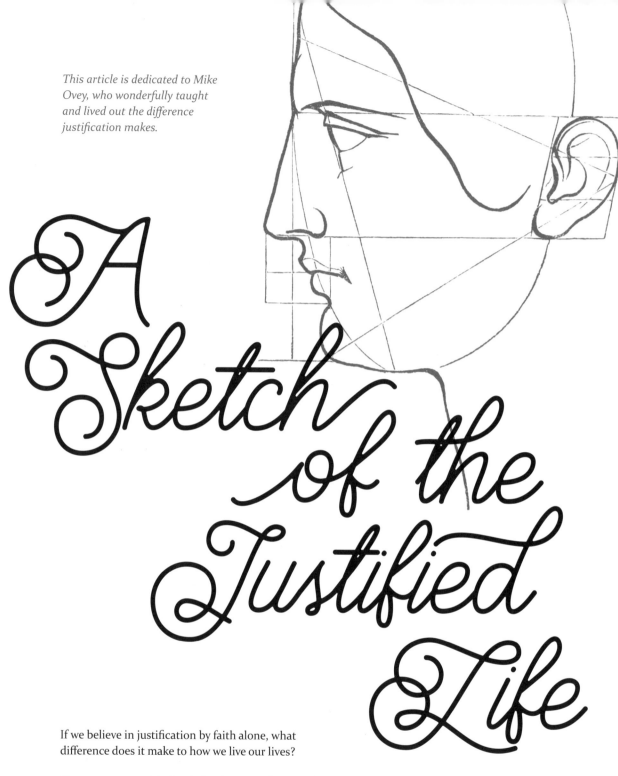

This article is dedicated to Mike Ovey, who wonderfully taught and lived out the difference justification makes.

A Sketch of the Justified Life

If we believe in justification by faith alone, what difference does it make to how we live our lives?

My answer, you might be glad to know, is that it makes a very great difference. Indeed it makes more of a difference in more areas of life than we often give it credit for. But as we begin we should recognise that other answers are available.

by David Shaw

First, there are some who would say justification makes no difference to how we live. In fact, it *cannot*. This has particularly been an argument made by people challenging the idea that justification is at the centre of Paul's theology. The thought is basically this:

- Paul's doctrine of justification "rejects not only the works of the Law, but works in general."

- If justification by faith preaches against good works then Paul "thus closes the pathway to a theory of ethics."

- Obviously, though, Paul *is* interested in people living good lives.

- Therefore, justification cannot be central and seems to be inconsistent with his overall aims for the churches.

Albert Schweitzer, *The Mysticism of Paul the Apostle*, trans. William Montgomery (London: A&C Black, 1931), 225. Likewise, Douglas Campbell takes the same view and for the same reason: "Justification theory famously struggles with ethics." *The Deliverance of God: An Apocalyptic Rereading of Justification in Paul* (Grand Rapids: Eerdmans, 2009), 80.

That might seem like quite a foreign debate but there is a form of it that often appears in churches. It is easy to teach justification in such a way that leaves people confused about whether they need to *do* anything and what role good works should play. At times, the desire to do good works has even been spoken of as inherently sinful – a legalistic attempt to stake a claim on God. In this view the only ethical value of the doctrine of justification is to teach us to believe and to be suspicious of any language about good works.

Second, some people would argue that believing the doctrine of justification by faith does make a difference, but not a positive one. Belief in justification signs us up for believing in a God who judges sin and condemns sinners. For many, that is a divisive and an offensive worldview to hold. And then there is the way in which the church has split over its understanding of justification, most notably at the Reformation but throughout the centuries since then as well. Even within the evangelical church, correctly stating and defending the doctrine of justification can become an exercise in hair-splitting, divisiveness, and prideful chest-beating. Put simply, some of the most vocal champions of justification by faith can sound very self-righteous. The effect, all too often, is that people can be wary of embracing or fine-tuning their understanding of justification because they don't want to become *that* sort of person.

So, belief in justification: a barrier to living well, or a cause of behaving badly. We will keep these in mind as we lay out the positive difference justification makes. To explore that difference, we will focus on Paul's letter to the Romans and then Luke's account of Jesus. Paul will provide us with the fullest sense of the difference justification makes. Luke will help us savour and visualise that difference.

Paul's letter to the Romans

Martin Luther, *Commentary on Romans* (trans. J. Theodore Mueller; Grand Rapids: Kregel, 1954), xiii.

For Luther, Paul's letter to the Romans "is worthy not only that every Christian should know it word for word, by heart, but occupy himself with it every day, as the daily bread of the soul." No doubt Luther's enthusiasm is largely due to the way in which Romans 1-8 sets out justification by faith, which it is worth summarising briefly.

Although there is no one who is righteous (3:10), and God's wrath is being poured out against human unrighteousness (1:18), God has nonetheless revealed a saving righteousness in the gospel through which all can be saved. In the death of Jesus the punishment for our unrighteousness has been borne by Jesus so that God can be both just (sin has not been swept under the carpet) and the one who justifies us (3:25-26). Crucially, this is a justification by *faith*. We have no works to offer. And as Paul shows in Romans 4, this is the way God has always related to his people. Both Abraham and David knew the justification of the ungodly, the forgiveness of their sins (4:1-8). It is a gift, freely given, as Paul is at pains to point out in 3:24 and 4:6-8.

It is also a gift that opens the door to other blessings. By the time we get to 5:1, Paul can address his audience as those who *have been* justified and start to lay out what life now looks like. Having been justified we have peace with God, access into the grace in which we now stand and we can boast in the hope of the glory to come. Indeed, we can even boast in sufferings because we know they can serve to increase that hope (5:1-5).

This confidence is grounded in the work of Jesus. He proves beyond doubt that God loves his people (5:6-11) and, just as surely as Adam unleashed sin and death on the world, so too has Jesus now unleashed righteousness and life (5:12-21).

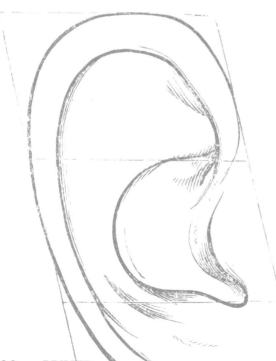

These things being true, Romans 6-8 then chart the ways in which we should now relate to sin (as our old slavemaster) and the extent to which we can walk in new ways of life. Paul makes clear that the law was not able to liberate people from sin (5:20-21, 7:5), but God, through Christ and the Spirit, has granted us freedom to walk in newness of life (6:1-14, 7:6, 8:1-4). That freedom, however, is a freedom to serve the Lord. As we once offered ourselves as slaves to sin, now we offer ourselves as slaves to righteousness (6:15-23). As we once lived according to the flesh, now we live according to the Spirit (8:5-12).

From this brief sketch we should note two things about the role of justification in Paul's argument.

First, it is the foundational blessing. *Having been justified* we have peace with God. Justification has this prior place, addressing the question of how unrighteous people can justly be accepted by God instead of being condemned. What God has done in Jesus answers the question that has rumbled all the way through the Old Testament – how can God dwell in the midst of a sinful people? How can God redeem his people when Jerusalem is filled with unrighteousness (Isaiah 1:21)? As Isaiah foresaw, the answer comes in God's promise to act, raining down his righteousness on his people: *you who are far from righteousness: I bring near my righteousness; it is not far off, and my salvation will not delay* (Isaiah 46:12-13, cf. 33:5 45:8). This is what Paul now announces in his gospel. If then we want to think about justification within Paul's theology, we have to say it is central to it in the way that a door is central to a house. It is the way in.

Second, and implicit in what we've just said: justification isn't the whole house. It is the "gateway blessing," but it doesn't have to do all the work. Paul can speak about how our works play no part in making us acceptable before God, but then, having established our justification by faith, he can go on to argue for ethical behaviour on other grounds.

Accordingly, this is a very common way of putting things in Reformed theology. For example, the *Heidelberg Catechism* puts it this way in Question 86:

> *Question: Since we have been delivered from our misery by grace through Christ without any merit of our own, why then should we do good works?*
>
> *Answer: Because Christ, having redeemed us by his blood, is also restoring us by his Spirit into his image, so that with our whole lives we may show that we are thankful to God for his benefits, so that he may be praised through us, so that we may be assured of our faith by its fruits, and so that by our godly living our neighbours may be won over to Christ.*

Our redemption consists of God's work on our behalf – freely justifying us but also transforming us by his Spirit to live in grateful enjoyment of the freedom we now have and conscious of the responsibilities we bear to God and neighbour. Or, in the common formula, sanctification follows justification. We have been put right with God and we are now being made more like Jesus.

In answer to that first objection then, that justification speaks against works and so cuts the nerve of ethics, we need to say no: Paul insists that works don't save and that saved people work. Within that basic framework, the doctrine of justification doesn't do all the heavy lifting, but no-one has ever suggested that it needs to. Generally speaking, justification refers to how we are made acceptable in the first place, and Paul discusses the Christian life more in the language of the Spirit, freedom, love and so on.

As an aside it is worth noting the way in which sanctification and justification language works in the Bible. Often we speak of justification as a definitive, once-for-all event, and sanctification as the ongoing transformation of believers. Properly speaking, though, both justification and sanctification refer to what God has done for us in Christ. We have been justified (legally acquitted) and we have been sanctified (set apart for the service and worship of God). For more on this see David Peterson, *Possessed by God: A New Testament Theology of Sanctification and Holiness* (Grand Rapids: Eerdmans, 1996).

Scripture clearly expects us to grow in Christlikeness, however, and we have often used the term 'sanctification' for this, distinguishing it from justification to guard against the thought that our justification is an ongoing process of renewal. This is helpful, so long as we remember David Starling's point that the Bible will sometimes use righteousness language to describe how we now live. The imputed righteousness of Christ has put us in the right with God, but we are called to offer our bodies and selves in the service of righteousness (Rom 6:13-14) and reminded that the kingdom of God is a matter of righteousness, peace and joy in the Holy Spirit (Rom 14:17).

On the other hand, it is notable that Paul often applies the truth of our justification by faith to the Christian life, and he does so in more ways than we often realise.

1. justification by faith and assurance

Rom 5:1 | *Therefore, since we have been justified through faith, we have peace with God through our Lord Jesus Christ.*

We are justified, and therefore at peace with the God who was rightly wrathful at our sin: the note of assurance here is loud and clear. Past justification establishes present peace and guarantees future salvation. As Rom 5:6-8 is at pains to emphasise, God justified us while we were his enemies, and so how much more can we be sure he will bring about our full and final salvation now that we are his friends. This was the great emphasis of Luther and Owen, as we have seen in previous articles. As people are conscious of their sin or approach their death we have a solid assurance to offer them that will quieten the conscience and assure the anxious.

What is perhaps less often seen is that the truth of justification also provides assurance in the face of opposition and hostility. Paul writes to the Romans very conscious that they will suffer. He introduces the theme in 5:2, returns to it in 8:18, and then again in 8:31-36:

Rom 8:31-36

> *If God is for us, who can be against us? He who did not spare his own Son, but gave him up for us all – how will he not also, along with him, graciously give us all things? Who will bring any charge against those whom God has chosen? It is God who justifies. Who then is the one who condemns? No one. Christ Jesus who died – more than that, who was raised to life – is at the right hand of God and is also interceding for us. Who shall separate us from the love of Christ? Shall trouble or hardship or persecution or famine or nakedness or danger or sword? As it is written:*
>
> *'For your sake we face death all day long; we are considered as sheep to be slaughtered.'*

In the face of opposition and suffering Paul appeals to God's unfailing love, just like Psalm 44, which he quotes here. But what Paul is specifically able to appeal to, now that Christ has come, is the clearest evidence that God does indeed love us (he did not spare his own Son), and to the fact that we have been justified in Christ. In the face of accusations, in all of life's little trial scenes, we know that the most important verdict has been spoken over us. It is *God* who justifies.

Not only does this thought free us from the fear of opposition, but also the pressure to prove ourselves to others. Justification by faith is one of the most potent doctrines to deal with the fear of man. It is also therefore the key to genuine love. If I am concerned with proving myself in human relationships then people will always be currency to me: The people whose opinions matter will be valuable and I will invest in them, but even then, only to make myself feel accepted; the people whose opinions don't matter to me will be brushed aside. But what if I take to heart the thought that I am justified by the one judge who really matters? I am now free to walk into room not sizing up the most advantageous conversation for me to start, but ready to serve and love others irrespective of whatever benefit I might think to gain.

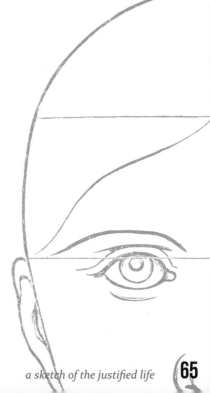

So justification, with the assurance it gives us, means we can face the future and endure opposition without fear. And it turns us outward to serve others. That is not all though. Paul's letter to the Romans puts justification by faith to work in at least a couple more ways. To see those, however, we need to step back for a moment and think about the purpose of Romans.

Although the letter is rightly thought of as Paul's fullest and most systematic statement of his theology, it is also closely connected to the situation of the Roman church on the one hand, and Paul's own situation on the other.

Paul has not visited the Roman church before. But he clearly knows enough about the church to know that there are some divisions within it over the question of what is acceptable to eat (14:2) and whether certain days are more sacred than others (14:5). Paul is concerned that people know the truth about these things (he clearly signals that all foods are now clean and acceptable to eat – 14:2, 14:5) but he is more concerned that people avoid judging one another and do what leads to peace. This is no small thing either: he devotes much of Rom 14-15 to addressing this.

Paul also writes with his own travel plans in view. He hopes to visit Rome but then also to receive help from the Roman church to continue his church-planting mission on to Spain (15:23-24). Again, this is no small thing and it is not unrelated to Paul's hopes that the church will avoid divisions and work together for peace. We can see that in Romans 15:7-13 (arguably the climax of the letter) where Paul draws together a chain of OT quotes which foresee the inclusion of Jews and Gentiles into one worshipping community. Likewise, in Romans 15:8, Paul says that Jesus became a servant so that the promises to the Jews might be fulfilled and that the Gentiles might praise God for his mercy.

That vision of one united, worshipping community speaks to both of Paul's reasons for writing. He wants the church to catch this vision and so get behind his mission to Spain so that people there can join this people of God, worshipping him with one mind and one voice (15:6). And he wants the Roman church to embody that wider worshipping community, to be a microcosm of it, by putting aside their differences and their judgmentalism, and by pursuing peace. He wants *them* specifically to worship God with one mind and one voice (15:6).

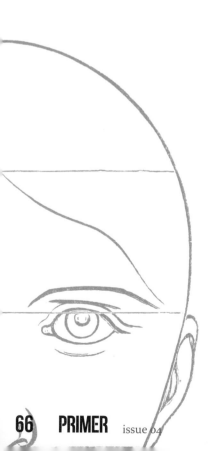

But what has this got to do with justification by faith? Much in every way. When we see the letter in this light, we can start to see how Paul has crafted his account of justification by faith in Romans 1-4 to encourage unity within the Roman church and support for the mission to Spain.

2. justification by faith and church unity

As we have seen, judgmentalism is a threat in Rome. The believers there are not to pass judgment on one another. To be sure, Paul offers some strong reasons for this within Rom 14-15 itself – for example, they will all appear before God's judgment seat in the future so they should not park themselves in that chair now, standing in judgment over others (14:10-12). But he has also laid a foundation for that argument throughout Romans 1-4. As Paul describes the world he makes it abundantly clear that there are no grounds for human boasting or one-upmanship. All of us have a common share in human unrighteousness:

> **Rom 3:9-10** *Jews and Gentiles alike are all under the power of sin. As it is written: "There is no one righteous, not even one..."*

And all of us have a common share in justification. Paul underlines these points and their relevance for church unity in three ways.

First, the language of 'all.' About 15 times in the first four chapters Paul emphasises that all are guilty and that the gospel is the power of salvation for all. You can see that flavour in Rom 3:22-23:

> **Rom 3:22-23** *This righteousness is given through faith in Jesus Christ to **all** who believe. There is no difference between Jew and Gentile, for **all** have sinned and fall short of the glory of God, and **all** are justified freely by his grace.*

Second, Paul explicitly takes aim at judgmentalism in Rom 2:1-4, the very issue he later confronts in Rom 14. Crucially he places it in the Rom 1-3 world: a world under God's judgment and a world of unrighteousness that unbelievers have supposedly left behind.

Third, there is the language of 'boasting.' Given this common share in unrighteousness and a salvation that none of us deserves, Paul asks "Where then is boasting?" (3:27). The answer: it is clearly excluded, "since there is only one God, who will justify the circumcised by faith and the uncircumcised through that same faith" (3:30).

Remarkably, though, boasting re-emerges in chapter 5 where Paul writes that we now boast in the hope we have (5:2), we glory (5:3, same word as before: we boast) in our sufferings, and we boast in God (5:11). But there is no whiff of self-righteousness in this boasting. The whole point is that we are boasting in what we have been graciously given through no merit of our own. Paul's whole point is that we cannot set ourselves over against anyone else because we have this common unrighteous past and this shared future. For this reason we should lament that there are some who speak about justification by faith in a self-righteous tone, as if their grasp of the doctrine sets them apart from the rest in some way. But we would also have to say that they have not understood justification by faith if it produces anything in them other than humility and a sense of sympathy with others.

Hopefully it is not hard to see how this would transform church life. Justification by faith means that nothing about me saved me, and nothing about you should shock me. Humility and inclusivity. "Accept one another, then, just as Christ has accepted you" (Rom 15:7). That is, irrespective of our past, our background, our ethnicity, our class, or our sexuality. Tragically that is not always the case, and the author Rosaria Butterfield puts her finger on why as she describes people's shocked reactions to her lesbian past, asking her whether she had "to tell people about *this*."

Rosaria Champagne Butterfield, *The Secret Thoughts of an Unlikely Convert* (Pittsburgh: Crown & Covenant, 2012), 138.

This. Rosaria's unmentionable past. Rahab the Harlot. Mary Magdalene. We love these women between the pages of our Bible, but we don't want to sit at the Lord's Table with them – with people like me – drinking from a common cup. That's the real ringer: the common cup – that is, our common origin in depravity. We are only righteous in Christ and in him alone. But that's a hard pill to swallow, especially if you give yourself kudos for good choices.

There is much food for thought here: how might our relationships, networks, and church-planting strategies either reinforce a mutually-held assumption that we are the 'right kind of people', or how might they embody the acceptance of all who might take the bread and drink the cup?

3. justification by faith and mission

We have already seen how Paul uses 'all' language to show that there is no difference between us. Jesus saves us without distinction, irrespective of our class, ethnicity, sexual past, or anything else. But Paul also uses that 'all' language to foster support for his mission to Spain. If the world is under God's wrath for its unrighteousness and ungodliness, and if the gospel "is the power of God for the salvation of all who believe: first the Jew, then the Gentile," then Paul's mission becomes vital.

My translation.

Equally, if Jesus' own mission was shaped by a desire to create that worshipping community from both Jews and Gentiles (15:8-9), then the Roman church must get behind that mission. This is one of the crucial things to see from Romans 4. Paul begins by showing that Abraham and David were themselves justified by faith – they were the ungodly who knew the blessing of being reckoned righteous by faith instead of having their sins reckoned to them. But from 4:9 Paul focuses on the scope of that blessing – is it for the Jews only, or also for the uncircumcised? As he clearly demonstrates, God's promise to Abraham was that he would be at the head of a worldwide family of faith. He is "the father of us all" (4:16) – the unity point again! – but he is also the "heir of the world" (4:13) and "the father of many nations" (4:18) – so get behind Paul's mission.

For more on Romans 4 and its implications for justification, see David A. Shaw, "Romans 4 and the Justification of Abraham in Light of Perspectives New and Newer," *Themelios* 40.1 (2015): 50–62.

Again, it is worth pausing to note that there is no room for self-righteousness here. Paul might remind his readers of the ways in which they participated in the world of unrighteousness in a way that distances them from those *behaviours*. They have made a decisive break from that way of life. But Paul won't let us forget that we were once just like the rest. He won't let us distance ourselves from those *people* as if we were somehow different or better. It's a point he makes most clearly in Titus 3:1-7, urging Titus to teach the people "to be ready to do whatever is good, to slander no one, to be peaceable and considerate, and always to be gentle towards everyone" (3:1-2).

And why? Because:

Titus 3:3-7

At one time we too were foolish, disobedient, deceived and enslaved by all kinds of passions and pleasures. We lived in malice and envy, being hated and hating one another. But when the kindness and love of God our Saviour appeared, he saved us, not because of righteous things we had done, but because of his mercy. He saved us through the washing of rebirth and renewal by the Holy Spirit, whom he poured out on us generously through Jesus Christ our Saviour, so that, having been justified by his grace, we might become heirs having the hope of eternal life.

"We too." It's a crucial thought that shows again the connection between justification by faith and humility. The only thing that sets us apart is the kindness and love and mercy of God; accordingly, what should set us apart in the world is that our good deeds reflect that kindness and love and mercy to the world.

Luke's portrait of Jesus

Paul is often given credit for the doctrine of justification, but it is clear that he would not claim that for himself. In part he would point us back to the Old Testament where we read of the righteous living by faith (Hab 2:4) and of course to Abraham in Gen 15:6 whose faith is credited as righteousness. But he would also say that the apostles shared a belief in justification by faith. Indeed that is what he does say to Peter, in the incident recorded in Galatians 2:11-21:

Gal 2:15-16
> We who are Jews by birth and not sinful Gentiles, know that a person is not justified by the works of the law, but by faith in Jesus Christ.

Paul is able to appeal to a doctrine of justification Peter and Paul have both held since their conversion. That is to say, from the earliest days of the NT church, they were speaking about the gospel in terms of justification by faith. Where did that come from? As we just said, the OT certainly played a part, but it is also likely that the teaching of Jesus lies behind this way of expressing it, not least the parable that Jesus tells in Luke 18:9-14:

Luke 18:9-14
> To some who were confident of their own righteousness and looked down on everyone else, Jesus told this parable: 'Two men went up to the temple to pray, one a Pharisee and the other a tax collector. The Pharisee stood by himself and prayed: "God, I thank you that I am not like other people – robbers, evildoers, adulterers – or even like this tax collector. I fast twice a week and give a tenth of all I get."
>
> 'But the tax collector stood at a distance. He would not even look up to heaven, but beat his breast and said, "God, have mercy on me, a sinner."
>
> 'I tell you that this man, rather than the other, went home justified before God. For all those who exalt themselves will be humbled, and those who humble themselves will be exalted.'

There is so much we could say about this passage, but I'll confine myself to two observations. First of all, notice the parallel with Paul. Jesus here describes a situation in which onlookers would assume that the Pharisee is righteous whereas the tax collector is not. Jesus' view, however, is that neither is righteous. For all his outward obedience, the Pharisee is looking down on everyone else and exalting himself. "No-one", as Paul might say, "is righteous" here, "no not one." And yet the remarkable punchline is that one of the men, simply by acknowledging his sin and crying out for mercy goes home justified, "freely by his grace" as Paul would surely add. So, Jesus and Paul are on the same page. And nor is this an isolated example. That last line of the parable, about the humble being exalted, is repeated word for word in Luke 14:11 and the thought occurs throughout the gospel making the same point: acceptance before God is a matter of seeking his mercy not earning his approval (see e.g. 1:46-55, 1:72, 16:14-15). Those who embrace that are included; those who resist it are excluded. As F.F. Bruce suggests, the parable of the Prodigal Son strikes exactly this note, with echoes of Paul:

It was Mike Ovey who helped me, and many others, to see this theme in Luke.

Paul and Jesus (London: SPCK, 1977), 54.

When the black sheep of the family came home in disgrace and started off with the fine speech he had so carefully rehearsed, his father might easily have said "That's all very well, young man we have heard fine speeches before. Now you buckle to and work as you have never worked in your life, and if we see that you really mean what you say we may let you work your passage. But first you must prove yourself; we can't let bygones be bygones as though nothing had happened." Even that would have done the young man a world of good, and even the elder brother might have consented to let him be placed on probation. And that is very much like some people's idea of God. But it was not Jesus' way of presenting God – nor was it Paul's.

For – and here is where the Pauline doctrine of justification comes in – God does not treat us like that. He does not put us on probation to see how we shall turn out – although, if he did so, that in itself would be an act of grace. But then we should never be really satisfied that we had made the grade, that our performance was sufficiently creditable to win the divine approval at the last. Even if we did the best we could – and somehow we do not always manage to do that – how could we be sure that our best came within measurable distance of God's requirement? We might hope, but we could never be certain. But if God in sheer grace assures us of our acceptance in advance, and we gladly embrace that assurance, then we can go on to do his will from the heart as our response of love, without constantly worrying whether we are doing it adequately or not.

Second, notice the ethics of justification. Too often we can sound like the Pharisee, looking down on other people for not being quite as orthodox as us, or for not belonging to our particular tribe, even while we talk about justification by faith. But we need to recognise this as the ethics of self-righteousness in all of it its divisive and proud ugliness. In stark contrast we see the ethics of justification by faith embodied in two places. First, in those who embrace it, the humble who find themselves lifted up. Justification by faith produces humility, it produces worship – expressed in Mary's song in Luke 1 and the extravagant act of the sinful woman (Luke 7:36-38), and it produces generosity, as witnessed by Zacchaeus (19:1-10). Second, we see the ethics of justification by faith in the person of Jesus himself. As he commissions his disciples in anticipation that "repentance for the forgiveness of sins will be preached in his name to all nations, beginning at Jerusalem," Luke would point us back to his model; to the way his interactions and mealtimes have embodied the kind of welcome and acceptance we should now show to others. Those encounters paint in technicolour what it will look like for us to "accept one another, just as Christ accepted you."

Conclusion

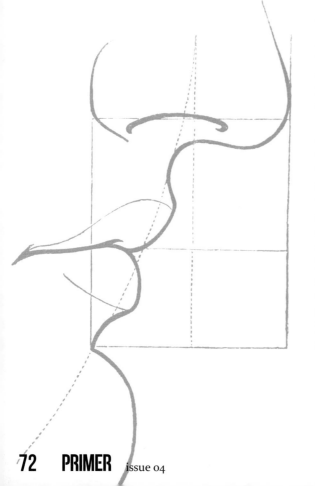

In summary, then, if we take our justification to heart, it will be a transformative truth. At a personal and corporate level it fuels assurance, perseverance, worship, humility, unity, and a compassionate concern for the lost. Properly speaking, justification itself speaks of the way in which human beings are put right with God. But as Paul and Jesus both show, the circumstances of our justification have all kinds of implications for the ways in which we treat one another.

As we seek to bring those implications to bear on the church, it is well worth reading on for Steve Timmis' wisdom. For my part, I'll just make one closing suggestion: Preach the gospel from the gospels. I know that when we think of justification or when we plan sermons to celebrate the Reformation we naturally turn to Romans or Galatians. But the gospels are worth turning to. In those parables and encounters we get living, breathing illustrations of what it looks like to embrace or reject the truth that God justifies the ungodly. We get to see what it looks for that truth to transform one life at a time; a socially despised woman here, a tax collector there. We glimpse the humility and the joy and the worship of the justified life. **P**

It is an answer to the greatest personal question ever asked by a human soul – the question,

"How shall I be right with God?"

...There are those, I admit, who never raise that question; there are those who are concerned with the question of their standing before men but never with the question of their standing before God; there are those who are interested in what 'people say' but not in the question of what God says.

Such men, however, are not those who move the world: they are apt to go with the current; they are apt to do as others do; they are not the heroes who change the destinies of the race.

The beginning of true nobility comes when a man ceases to be interested in the judgment of men and becomes interested in the judgment of God.

J. Gresham Machen
from a sermon called 'Justified by Faith'

Cosmically Joyful

In this final article we want to think more explicitly about how to communicate the truth of justification: Should we always mention it when we present the gospel? What are the objections we need to deal with? How can we illustrate it well? We put these and other questions to Steve Timmis.

 **How does justification relate to 'the gospel' and 'salvation'? And so how prominent should justification be in our preaching?**

These terms need working definitions if we are to see how they relate to each other. *The gospel* is all that God has done for us in Christ and all that he has for us in Christ. *Salvation* is a comprehensive term describing God's past, present and future action on our behalf as needy sinners.

If these working definitions have any validity, clearly they are very close to one another. The gospel is good news because it declares that God has acted on our behalf to rescue us from both our sin and his righteous judgment. This being so, then justification is an integral and necessary feature of them both. It is part of the gospel. It is the critical means by which we were saved, are being saved and will be saved. In fact, in order to underline the point, there is no gospel without the truth of justification. There is no salvation without justification.

This then raises the question as to the actual nature of justification. *The Westminster Shorter Catechism* (available in many places online) provides an excellent description in answer to Question 33:

 Justification is an act of God's free grace in which he pardons all our sins and accepts us as righteous in his sight for the sake of the righteousness of Christ alone, which is credited to us and received by faith alone.

This definition emphasises the fact that our justification flows out of God's free grace – it is his initiative, which he undertakes for us in Christ. Again, it shows the inseparable connection between justification, gospel and salvation.

But there is a word of caution. 'Rabbi' Duncan, the 18th century Scottish Presbyterian, pointed out that as critical as justification is, it is not the fundamental evangelical doctrine – Christ himself is. This requires us to see justification as part of a greater truth, namely, our union with Christ. It is only through a real and dynamic union with Christ that we actually shared in his death and resurrection. We are now able to live as those so justified because the wages of sin have been paid. It is this union, and this union alone, that allows us to participate in the great acts of Christ. From that firm basis we put to death our old self and live a new, justified life in union with him, through the indwelling power of the Spirit. The Spirit is the irrefutable testimony to, and demonstration of, our union.

This being so, the question about the prominence of justification in our preaching becomes essentially rhetorical. If the task of the preacher is to declare the whole counsel of God – to preach the gospel to both saints and sinners – then in some shape or form justification will be an ever-present truth.

Justification is God's answer to our sin and consequential judgment. The rehearsal of it is an indispensable provocation to godliness as we grapple with both our definitive and progressive sanctification. Nothing will so nurture the assurance of the believer as the faithful, passionate, applied preaching of justification. Sinclair Ferguson encapsulates its importance:

> *Assurance is nourished on a clear understanding of grace and especially of union with Christ and the justification, adoption, and regeneration that are ours freely in him... justification is both final and complete. It is final because it is the eschatological justification of the last day brought forward into the present day. It is complete because in justification we are counted as righteous before the Father as Christ himself, since the only righteousness with which we are righteous is Jesus Christ's righteousness. When faith thus grasps the reality of this inheritance, then Christ himself looms large. This is the key to the enjoyment of assurance precisely because assurance is our assurance that he is a great Saviour and that he is ours.*

Sinclair Ferguson, *The Whole Christ: Legalism, Antinomianism, and Gospel Assurance - Why the Marrow Controversy Still Matters* (Wheaton: Crossway, 2016), 200.

That is what we get to preach! Isn't that absolutely remarkable? What an immense privilege! I cannot think of anything I would rather tell a room full of marred and scarred men and women.

Look at how Luther so comprehensively shows justification answering the attacks of the devil:

> *When the devil throws our sins up to us and declares that we deserve death and hell, we ought to speak thus: 'I admit that I deserve death and hell. What of it? Does this mean that I shall be sentenced to eternal damnation? By no means. For I know One who suffered and made satisfaction in my behalf. His name is Jesus Christ, the Son of God. Where he is, there I shall be also.'*

Martin Luther, cited in Theodore G. Tappert, *Luther: Letters of Spiritual Counsel*, ed. Theodore G. Tappert (Vancouver: Regent College Publishing, 2003).

I wish I had space to show how justification addresses the problem of our fear of others, or how it provides an impetus to mission, or how it impacts our understanding of vocation and shapes our participation in community.

For more on this, see David Starling's article.

In fact, with respect to the participation in community, this is a good point at which to engage albeit briefly with the so-called New Perspective. To lay all my cards on the table, I don't think NT Wright et al are all wrong. This 'school' has highlighted some aspects that historically evangelicals have ignored and ought not to have done. Clearly, there are inherent dangers in the view, as shown by the enthusiasm with which many outside of confessional evangelicalism have embraced it. But I think the following statement articulates the individual and corporate nature of justification well:

> *RESOLVED – to be clear on what justification by faith actually means, which is a judicial declaration by God of our right standing before him and our simultaneous incorporation in the eschatological people of God solely on the basis of the completed cross-work of Jesus.*

Statement from Acts 29 Europe, Rome Conference, 2016.

two

How do we help unbelievers grasp the truth of justification? What cultural or presuppositional challenges are there?

One of the real challenges we face culturally is the **radical rejection of sin** as a category. Along with this goes the awareness of guilt, either objective or affective. In fact, anything encouraging people to think of themselves as guilty sinners is viewed as psychologically harmful. This is a problem we must navigate well and wisely. The reality is that we are sinners, and we all do experience guilt in some way, at various times. There is no-one, of any maturity, who does not have skeletons in the cupboard or demons whispering in their ears. It is to those who are weary and burdened that we speak the truth of what God has done for us and what he has for us in Christ. I think this is an important point to remember. As Jesus said, he did not come for the healthy. Now obviously, we know our doctrines well enough to know that there is no one who is healthy – so too did Jesus! He is saying that he is of no use nor interest to those who labour under delusions of being in good shape. Our role is to preach justification with the confidence that, through the power of the Holy Spirit, it will speak to those with ears to hear. It will be good news to those struggling with sin. It will be a healing gel to those who are wounded. It is not our task to make the truth relevant; it is our task to show its pertinence to the human condition. The point of connection we have is our shared humanity. Justification is a remarkable truth that speaks peace to the troubled soul.

Another cultural barrier is as old as Eden: **the inordinate desire to justify ourselves**. We want to be self-made men and women. We pursue that through relationships, charitable acts, niceness, happy families, careers, wealth – the list is endless. But whatever means we employ, self-justification will always fail. When that happens we have a couple of options. One is that we reconfigure our lives by rewriting our history; this acts as self-protection. A failed marriage is the fault of the unreasonable spouse; a bad review at work is the fault of the system or the incompetence of the manager... and so it goes. Alternatively, we acknowledge our failure and our part in it; this leaves us helpless, yet we still want to play the saviour. So we seek justification through naked hedonism – drinks, drugs, exercise, promiscuity. At these critical moments we can speak the beautiful truth of how Christ took on himself our sin, and of how the Father accepts his Son's work on our behalf.

We must not lose sight of the fact that justification, if understood rightly, is an offensive doctrine. This is because it is the great leveller. Paul shows this emphatically in Romans 3: *"There is no one righteous, not even one"* (v10). We cannot imagine that such a scathing indictment of the human condition will fail to incite the flesh!

Some other barriers include:

1   The assumption that the grounds of our justification (Jesus' punishment-bearing death) is barbaric like some form of cosmic child abuse.

2   The relinquishing of privileges attached to one's background, tradition, practices, achievements or status.

3   The hermeneutics of suspicion – the latent nihilism of 21st century Europe means that people have a hard job believing in something as hopeful, as cosmically joyful, as justification.

4   The presence of competing forces within the relics of Christendom – people are inoculated to the gospel and to justification because of the vestiges of Catholicism, for example.

5   The pluralist paradigm plays against Christian justification because the latter claims privilege and unique status for Christians.

6   The self-help market offers ways to feel good, have a positive self-image, even live wisely in the world; this militates against the needed bedrock of God's approval for human flourishing.

7   Justification by peer-group and Facebook "likes."

people

have a hard

job believing in

something

as hopeful, as

cosmically

joyful

as justification

three

What advice would you give to preachers trying to illustrate the truth of justification? Which illustrations do you find most helpful or unhelpful?

I would encourage every preacher to work very hard at illustrating this compelling truth. Our job is to not only make the truth plain, but also to make it a felt reality. Find ways to show the consequences of believing we are justified on the grounds of anything other than Christ's righteousness imputed to us: bring the crushing burden of self-justification into clear focus. Then open wide the window of true doctrine, so that the life-giving breath of grace in Christ can refresh. Teach the difference between intellectual and functional belief, with prayerfulness and humility. Luther used marriage as an illustration:

> "
>
> *Therefore a man can with confidence boast in Christ and say: 'Mine are Christ's living, doing, and speaking, his suffering and dying, mine as much as if I had lived, done, spoken, suffered, and died as he did.' Just as a bridegroom possesses all that is his bride's and she all that is his – for the two have all things in common because they are one flesh – so Christ and the church are one spirit.*

Martin Luther, "Two Kinds of Righteousness".

The courtroom image is well-tried, and given the essential forensic nature of justification it is very useful. But the illustration I return to most often when I'm speaking with Christians is our attitude to prayer. Are we hesitant to pray because we are aware of specific sin? Or are we eager in prayer because we are aware of a particular achievement? Either way, we're relying on something other than the finished work of Christ on our behalf. Again we face the offence of justification: because I am *in Christ*, I have neither more nor less right to speak with my Father on the basis of my performance – no matter how commendable or reprehensible it may have been.

four

If you could recommend only one newer book and one older book on justification, what would they be?

I confess to feeling a little short-changed in being allowed only two books, but if that's how it is, here they are:

Faith and its Evidences by John Owen. If you get through the Latin quotes and his complicated sentence structure, it's a goldmine.

The Whole Christ: Legalism, Antinomianism and Gospel Assurance - Why the Marrow Controversy Still Matters by Sinclair Ferguson. Basically, my rule of thumb is: if Sinclair has written it, it's worth me buying it! **P**